11/17/10

PAT,
HOPE YOU ENJOY THIS
BOOK ABOUT SOME OF
MY LOCAL BUDDIES
BEST WISHES

Jerry Whiting

Veterans in the Mist

World War II Memoirs of the Third
Thursday Lunch Bunch

Veterans in the Mist

World War II Memoirs of the Third
Thursday Lunch Bunch

Jerry W. Whiting

Veterans in the Mist
Copyright © 2010 by Jerry Whiting

Edited by: Dr. Elliott S. Dushkin and LizAnn Fulgham

Book Design and Printing by Falcon Books

San Ramon, California

ISBN 978-0-9713538-4-8

Library of Congress Control Number: 2010928294

Published by
TARNABY
2576 Fox Circle
Walnut Creek, CA. 94596
EAJWhiting@aol.com

PRINTED IN THE UNITED STATES OF AMERICA

Table of Contents

Acknowledgments

The author is grateful for the assistance of all who helped, in various ways, to produce this book. Most are listed below. Some of those who provided encouragement and inspiration are not on this list, but are not forgotten.

Armstrong, William
Bailey, Richard
Boswell, Louis
Brenner, Sy
Bybee, John and SPG
Cram, Steve
Debono, Ken
Denny, Herman
Dushkin, Lee
Ezersky, John
George Fries
Al Groeper
Gilcrest, John
Guevera, Joe
Guevara, Joyce
Harris, Paul
Jensen, Warren
Jones, Vernon

Lascotte, Mark
Lisica, Sime
Looker, Neil
McKay, Bob
Morgan, Tom
Orschiedt, Helmuth
Parrish, Fonzie
Posey, Larry
Robinson, Harry
Sanders, Sandy
Satz, Lou
Slominski, Jean
Slominski, Ray
Tharratt, Robert
Timmers, Aileen
Timmers, Frank
Turkington, Martin
Whiting, Ann

Foreword

Being born in 1942 and growing up in the Chicago suburb of Mt. Prospect, I remember the World War II veterans as they came marching home victoriously from the war. My older brother and I would visit a neighbor and ask him to tell us "war stories". I can imagine now how he must have modified his memories to address his young audience, who were still riding tricycles around the neighborhood. I have to admit that it was like visiting with Santa Claus and he even gave us some tattered ribbons and patches that I cherish to this day. He was a true war hero in my mind.

Sixty plus years have passed at the speed of life and now I am a veteran myself, of the Vietnam War. Upon graduating from college in Michigan, I, too, entered the U.S. Army through the ROTC program and found myself marching off to war as a helicopter pilot into what sounded like a true boyhood adventure. Somehow the Korean War had slipped by while I was growing up. I served in the active and reserve forces for a short 30 years of our great nation's history.

Now retired, both as an Army officer and commercial airline pilot, I find myself doing volunteer jobs in my areas of expertise, primarily aviation. Thus, one day I found myself at an EAA (Experimental Aircraft Association) board meeting, being asked to find some veterans who served on the B-17 aircraft so they could be offered the first ride when the aircraft came to the local airport.

I was able to locate two local men who had served on the B-17 in Europe, one as a pilot and one as a turret gunner. It was like striking gold and it quickly took me back so many years to those boyhood memories. The ball turret gunner, Bob Tharratt, was one of those riders and was emotionally moved by the experience. The last time he had flown in a B-17 was the day he bailed out of a crippled aircraft over Europe and became a POW. Bob became a friend and invited me to meet with the "Third Thursday" gang at a local restaurant. What a treat it has been to meet and listen to the stories of these brave men!

The World War II veterans are still with us and walk amongst us every day. You might catch a glimpse of one during a Memorial Day, Veterans Day, or Fourth of July parade. They are our great nation's golden treasures and if you should have the honor to meet one, shake his or her hand and thank them for their service to our country.

My friend Jerry Whiting has captured in his third book some of the stories of these great American patriots. Enjoy these stories and witness firsthand how each of these warriors saved the world from tyranny during World War II.

Richard A. Sperling, DSC
Col. (Ret) Aviation Branch, U.S. Army
Historian, Legion of Valor

■ ■ ■ ■ ■ ■ ■ ■ ■ ■

Prologue

They start filtering in about 11 am, like clockwork, on the third Thursday of every month. Most patrons at the Denny's Restaurant in Concord, California don't even notice them when they enter. The meeting doesn't start until 11:30, but these men are punctual. They don't wait to be seated, but walk directly to the banquet room in the back of the restaurant.

Some are pretty spry; others walk slowly. A few use canes or walkers for balance. This is not a group of young men. The youngest are in their mid 80's and the oldest is 96; still they come. It's extremely unusual to see fifty or more men in this age group gathered anywhere, for any reason.

The restaurant manager greets them as they walk past the reception area. The waitresses know them on sight and exchange pleasantries as the men join their buddies. Some have a favorite table or booth; others sit where it's convenient. Conversations begin immediately in small groups. Many of these men wear hearing aids so the conversations tend to be louder than normal.

Occasionally a patron will notice the group gathering in the banquet room and asked a waitress who they are. The waitress will explain that this is a special group of World War II veterans who meet every month. Once in a while someone much younger will enter the banquet room to thank one or two of them. More often a customer will approach one of the men when he is leaving, to chat and to offer thanks. The recipient of the gratitude will smile, somewhat surprised, perhaps a little embarrassed, but honored. Thanks? For what? The thanks are for the freedoms we have today. These men are World War II vets and collectively, they saved the world.

Oddly enough, it all began with a cross. No one would have thought in their wildest dreams that what started with such a humble beginning would grow from a core group of five vets to monthly luncheon meetings where 60-plus men gather.

The cross was the Distinguished Flying Cross. On November 11, 2000 Bob Tharratt received the Distinguished Flying Cross at the annual Veterans Day ceremony in Walnut Creek, California. He received the award for saving the life of a fellow crewman when their B-17 was shot down over Nuremberg, Germany on September 10, 1944. Bob, a ball turret gunner, buckled a parachute on the wounded crewman and helped him bail out of the stricken aircraft. The story did not surface until years later in a conversation with Gary Villalba, a Veteran Service Officer at the V.A. Medical Center in Martinez, California.

Villalba believed strongly that Bob should be honored for his life-saving efforts so many years ago and took it upon himself to begin the long process for this recognition. Hundreds of people were present when Bob was presented the Distinguished Flying Cross and the POW medal by Colonel Jack Peters, United States Air Force. It was one of the proudest day of his life. Normally, it would have ended there, except for the phone calls.

Bob received a phone call from Ray Slominski, another former ball turret gunner, also a former POW, who read a newspaper article about Bob and the award. Yet another former ball gunner, Ralph Brehl, phoned and so did Marvin Johnson, a former tail gunner. Frank Tiscareno, a retired police officer and Army veteran from the 1950's, wrote a poem about Bob and presented it to him.[1]

Original "Lunch Bunch"-early 2001 photo (L-R): Ray Slominski, Bob Tharratt, Frank Tiscareno, Marvin Johnson, Ralph Brehl (R. Slominski)

It was Ray Slominski who suggested they meet for lunch and this was the beginning. They met at a small restaurant in Walnut Creek. They had so much to talk about and had such an enjoyable experience that Ray suggested they meet monthly and bring any other World War II Vets who were interested. The others agreed and this became a regular event for them.

The group grew in numbers, slowly at first.[2] Ray talked to his many friends who were World War II veterans and some of them began attending. Within just a few months the group had outgrown the small restaurant and moved to a larger restaurant in Walnut Creek that had a separate room for them to meet. In less than a year, the average monthly group attendance had grown to more than 20 men. Ralph Brehl took it upon himself to make a roster of attendees and to make a reminder phone call to the men a few days before the meeting.

Often there was no agenda. The men just gathered to enjoy one another's company. Although the group started with former Army Air Force vets, men from all branches of service were welcome. There was no chairman, no rules of order, no bylaws, no dues, nothing to suggest a formal organization; yet they came.

Occasionally guest speakers were invited to speak at the luncheon. Sometimes it was an author or someone on active military duty. One such guest speaker was an orphan whose father was killed in World War II; another was a retired FBI agent and yet another worked at the Concord Vet's Center. Once in a while a member gave a presentation on his own personal experiences. Mostly the men just visited at the meetings. There was no publicity and no formal announcements of the meetings in local newspapers. It was all word of mouth and the group continued to grow.

The room where the vets met had a capacity of 30 people and sometimes that many attended. With a full room it was becoming difficult for some of the men to move around, particularly whose with canes or walkers. The restaurant closed about the same time the group needed a larger room. A search began for another restaurant that would allow the group to meet regularly. It was difficult finding a centrally-located restaurant that would allow the men to meet and accommodate the men having separate checks. This was a primary requirement. The Denny's Restaurant in Concord welcomed the group and offered a banquet room with a large seating capacity.

The group continues to grow. There are several attendees who are younger and who attend to honor the World War II Vets. Some served in other wars in Korea, Vietnam and the Persian Gulf or served in peacetime, but the group remains about, and for, World War II Vets.

They come from all walks of life, of every race, from a variety of religious backgrounds and from different political parties. Some had a military career, but most were citizen soldiers, serving at a time when their country needed them most, and went on to have careers and serve their communities in other capacities. There have been attendees from all branches of the military. There are former doctors, lawyers, factory workers, mechanics, salesmen, realtors and teachers in the group, to list just a few of their past careers. They live locally now, but come from nearly every state. A few were born in other countries. Some belong to several organizations; some belong to no other groups. The one thread that brings them together is that they served our country in World War II.

This is primarily a mens group. On occasion there is a female guest, usually a wife or daughter, but the regular attendees are men. This is just the way it is.

Ray Slominski, the inspiration for the regular meetings, died in 2006. Bob Tharratt worried that the group couldn't continue without Ray. He needn't have worried. Others stepped in to help with the planning. Occasionally the group gets some publicity, but they don't ask for it. The roster of World War II veterans who attend the meeting continues to grow, despite the fact that statistically, their numbers are decreasing. Some of the men don't drive anymore, but are brought to the meetings by others in the group or by wives or friends. The meetings are important to them.

There are more formal presentations at the meetings now. Outside speakers are sometimes invited, but most of the speakers are from within the group. They are encouraged to speak of their own experiences during the war. These personal accounts are welcomed by the group and more of them are openly sharing their experiences. It's a safe place to do so. Their audience understands.

Some members talk openly about their World War II experiences, while others are more reluctant. Some share little information about their service, aside from basic information about their branch of service, when introductions are made. Some have

Ray Slominski and Bob Tharratt at early lunch (R. Slominski)

extensive combat experience and some never went overseas. One never hears the "H" word in this group, the word hero. That's not what this group is about.

Due to the increase in group size, there are now several volunteers who make the monthly reminder calls. A retired Navy veteran who served during the Korean and Vietnam wars, Verle Hendrickson, videotapes the meetings. Others help with planning the meetings and keeping the roster up to date. It's a group effort, without any formal organization. It just gets done.

Another group has formed behind the scenes to honor the group. Informally they call themselves "Friends of the Third Thursday Lunch Bunch" and they have provided luncheons and barbecues for the men (and sometimes for the wives), usually around the holidays. The group wants no attention or recognition. They don't regularly attend the meetings, but they've chosen to honor the "Lunch Bunch" in this way.

Each and every one of these vets answered the call when their country needed them. Many paid a heavy price for their service. They served on all battlefields and represent every campaign fought in World War II. All lost friends who paid the ultimate price for the freedom we enjoy today and they haven't forgotten.

To look at them in passing, one would think they are just a group of senior citizens, perhaps a group of grandfathers and great grandfathers, and take no further notice. They don't stand out and they don't draw attention to themselves. We must look more closely so we see them clearly for who they are and what they have done for us. There are important lessons to learn from them, but we have to look past the surface, beyond the mist of decades of life's experiences, to see them clearly. We owe it to them and to our great nation.

1. See Frank Tiscareno's poem in Appendix.

2. Sadly, Frank Tiscareno was killed in an automobile accident in April 2001, shortly after the group began meeting. Marvin Johnson moved out of the area within a year. Ralph Brehl died in 2009.

■ ■ ■ ■ ■ ■ ■ ■ ■ ■

Chapter 1

An Adventure Gone Awry

I t began as a father and son outing, one of those early boyhood experiences that could later turn into a wonderful memory for 4 ½ year-old Steve Cram. It ended much differently.

Steve was born on the island of Maui, Hawaii and lived with his parents and infant brother in Kahului. Steve's father, Harold, was a minister in the Congregational church. They lived in a nice home supplied by the church, right on the beach. He didn't have a church of his own, but was the head of the Maui Conference of Churches. Pastor Cram received an invitation to attend a dinner banquet and to give the blessing at the Tripler Army Hospital on the nearby island of Oahu. Mrs. Cram was pregnant with their third child and was unable to accompany the pastor, so he decided to take Steve with him. It would be an adventure for the young boy and an opportunity for them to spend time together. They could also visit cousins. Pastor Cram accepted the invitation to the banquet, to be held on December 5, 1941.

Father and son took the intra-island steamer to Oahu and got off at the port in Honolulu on the date of the banquet. The boat ride took several hours and young Steve felt queasy on the

journey. He felt much
better after they docked
and came ashore. Their
cousins met them at the
pier. Later in the day the
cousins gave them a ride
to the banquet at Tripler
Hospital, which sits high
on Maunalua Ridge, over-
looking Honolulu. It was a
thrill for Steve to see the
Army, Navy, and Marine
officers all dressed in their
formal uniforms. Pastor
Cram gave the dinner
blessing for the large
group of military person-
nel assembled and they

Pastor Harold Cram and Steve in 1940
or early 1941 (S. Cram)

enjoyed a nice dinner. They left shortly after dinner. After all, in
those days it wasn't proper for a pastor to join in the socializing
and dancing that occurred later that evening. They returned to
their cousin's home to spend the night.

The next day was theirs and they spent the day relaxing and
socializing with the cousins. Pastor Cram was invited to assist a
Navy chaplain the next day at the Sunday morning worship service aboard the *USS Solace*, a Navy hospital ship moored at the
nearby Navy base at Pearl Harbor. They retired to their relative's
house early Saturday night, because Sunday was going to be a
long day. Steve was excited at the prospect of seeing all the ships.

On Sunday morning they were up very early. A cousin gave
them a ride to the entrance to the Navy base. The base was
guarded, but Pastor Cram received special permission to enter.
Normally civilians weren't allowed at the military installation.
Steve was impressed. The Navy chaplain met them at the gate

and the three of them walked to the pier together. Steve could barely contain his excitement. He had never seen so many ships in one place. It was a thrilling experience for the young boy. They were met by a small motorboat at the pier, manned by a single sailor and taken to the *USS Solace*, anchored in the harbor. It was a big, magnificent ship, painted white with a green cross and green markings. Since they were early they were given a tour of the ship. The sailors paid a lot of attention to the boy and Steve decided right then and there that he wanted to be a ship's captain. Soon it was time for Pastor Cram to change into his robe and prepare for the church service, set to begin at 8:00 am.

It was a few minutes before 8 am when the chaplain, Pastor Cram and Steve began walking through the ship on their way to the chapel. They never made it. Suddenly there were planes flying overhead and explosions in the distance. The noise was deafening! It seemed as if there were hundreds of them! Pearl Harbor was under attack! The chaplain reacted quickly and grabbed the pastor and Steve, pushing them towards the port side of the stern of the ship, urging them to hurry. Steve heard the sound of

USS Solace (U.S. Navy)

machineguns and explosions and looked up to see smoke in the distance.

When they reached the stern port side, a couple of levels below the main deck, the chaplain urged them to get quickly into a small motorboat, the same one that brought them to the *Solace*, manned by the same seaman. They jumped into the launch and immediately pulled away from the big ship and headed for the pier. Steve smelled and saw oil and gasoline on the water's surface. The sky seemed full of planes and bombs were exploding. As they motored toward the pier Steve saw a huge explosion on a big battleship moored across the bay, followed by smoke and flames.[1] As they pulled alongside the pier, Steve looked across the harbor and saw the water in the distance was now ablaze and the flames were coming toward them. Steve's father lifted him onto the ladder. He yelled "Run as fast as you can! Run!" and Steve and his father both ran down the pier. Steve looked back and saw the wall of flames still coming in the direction of the pier.

The sounds of powerful, screaming aircraft engines, machinegun fire, exploding torpedoes and bombs combined with the yells of sailors running in various directions, the sight and smells of burning ships, all added to the chaos and pandemonium. Steve had never seen his father in such a hurry and they continued running, reaching the main gate in just a few minutes. It was frightening and both were exhausted. There were people and cars everywhere, some entering, some leaving. Pastor Cram flagged down a passing vehicle when they reached the main road to Honolulu. Two Hawaiian men in the car picked them up. Steve and his dad got into the backseat of the car and they drove off. It was a relief to get away from the besieged naval base.

The men took them to Aloha Tower, the lighthouse at Honolulu harbor. They were several miles from Pearl Harbor now and it was quieter. The noise was gone and the only evidence of the nearby carnage was smoke rising in the distance. Some of the local citizenry didn't even realize what had occurred. There was little information available on the radio until several hours later. Pastor Cram went to local shops and finally located a phone to call the cousins and let them know they were safely away from the naval base. There was no way to contact Steve's mother.

Captain Steve Cram in Germany circa 1962 (S. Cram)

By early afternoon Martial law had been declared. In the distance Steve saw more smoke rising from the direction of the harbor, evidence of the final Japanese attack on the island. By mid-afternoon, the radio stations were providing preliminary information about the attack and the military was taking control of the island. Everything was being locked down. It looked as if no one would be leaving the island.

Pastor Cram wanted to get back to his wife and family in Maui as quickly as possible. He started talking to the Japanese fishermen who were tending to their boats in the harbor and finally found one who lived on Maui and also wanted to get back to his family. They decided to wait until dark and take a chance on crossing to the nearby island at night. When it was completely dark, the three of them left in the small, motor-driven fishing boat. They couldn't risk having any running lights on the boat. Steve was seasick and miserable for the entire journey, which took several hours. He quickly lost the enthusiasm he had earlier in the day to become a ship's captain.

Steve Cram-recent photo
(Author's collection)

They finally pulled into the harbor at Kahului during the early morning hours. The pastor and Steve walked the short distance to the beachfront home where the Cram family lived. It had been a memorable father and son trip, but it certainly wasn't the sort of experience Pastor Cram wanted etched in his son's memory.

Due to the fear of a Japanese attack, church officials moved the Cram family further inland for the remainder of the war. After high school, Steve attended San Francisco State College and U.C. Berkeley.[2] During the Vietnam War he served in the U.S. Army as a helicopter pilot at Saigon Hospital. He received his medical degree from U.C.S.F. and served as a medical examiner in San Francisco and retired more than 20 years of service. He later obtained a PhD in music from Northwestern University and is currently the music director at Grace Presbyterian Church in Walnut Creek, California. He resides in San Francisco.[3]

(Author's note: The USS Solace *was not damaged during the attack on Pearl Harbor. Its launches and crew rescued and treated sailors from the* USS Arizona *and* USS West Virginia, *as well as assisting a salvage party at the* USS Oklahoma.*)[4]*

NOTES

1. When Steve was older he learned the ship he witnessed explode was the Arizona.

2. San Francisco State is now California State University San Francisco

3. The author interviewed Steve Cram on 4/9/10 in Walnut Creek, California and re-interviewed him on 4/15/10.

4. This information is from the action report of the *USS Solace*, CINCPAC action report Serial 0479 of 15 February 1942, National Archives and Records Administration.

■ ■ ■ ■ ■ ■ ■ ■ ■ ■

Chapter 2

The Day after Infamy

The attack on Pearl Harbor on December 7, 1941 has become widely known as the "Date that will live in Infamy", a term used by President Franklin Roosevelt when he addressed Congress the next day. When the attack occurred, across the International Date Line in the Philippines, it was already Monday, December 8th.

On that day Harry Robinson, a 13 year-old boy, was getting ready for school at his family home near Nichols Field, an American airbase 10 miles south of Manila, on the island of Luzon. Harry and his family were American citizens, although Harry was born in the Philippines. He lived a comfortable middle class lifestyle with his parents, two brothers and three sisters.[1] His father worked for the U.S. Rubber Company. He was listening to the family Philco console radio when he heard a broadcast that Pearl Harbor had been attacked by the Japanese. Although the news was disconcerting, it wasn't worrisome for the young teenager and he finished preparing for school.

Harry's father drove the children to school like he did every morning before he went to work, a 15-minute drive from their home. When Harry arrived at Central Bordner High School

Robinson family 1940 or early 1941. Harry is in the middle-front row
(H. Robinson)

where he was a freshman, there was confusion everywhere. His father didn't just drop him off at school this day, but stayed with him to see what was going to happen at the school. This attack in the Hawaiian Islands was obviously a matter of great concern for the teachers. It was a very disorganized situation and the teachers didn't know how to respond. School was finally canceled and Harry returned home with his father. At noon that day Clark Field, an airbase 65 miles north of Manila, was attacked by Japanese bombers. To young Harry this was all very interesting, but was still no cause for worry. He thought the Americans would win in just a few days.

That night around 3 am he was awakened by loud explosions! The Japanese were bombing nearby Nichols Field, less than a mile from his home. Gasoline storage tanks were set afire by the bombing.[2] This was getting more interesting now, but he was still not worried. There was a major American military presence in the Philippines, with thousands of soldiers, airmen and sailors stationed nearby to defend the islands. The next morning his father went to work, as usual, and Harry found pieces of shrapnel on the ground from the early morning bombing. He wouldn't attend school again until this war issue could get resolved. Compounding the problem was that very little information was available. Rumors abounded, with few facts available.

Within a couple of days there was an addition to the local scenery on the Robinson property after U.S. Army soldiers came to his house and set up a .30 caliber machinegun in the backyard. The house was on the route of the Japanese bombing and strafing attacks against Nichols Field, which were now becoming regular, generally around noon. The Japanese planes flew over in "V" formations, in flights of three or six. This was getting to be quite an adventure now for young Harry.

A week after the attack, Harry's mother, who didn't look at these events as an adventure, put her foot down and said something must be done. She thought it was getting too dangerous and someone was going to get hurt if they stayed in their home. Harry's father decided to move the family to Manila in order to get away from the bombings. They quickly packed up and moved to an apartment in Manila. By this time the Japanese had started to invade the Philippines at several different locations and the bombings continued. There were still lots of rumors, but little accurate information available. His father continued going to work, while Harry and his siblings stayed at home during the day.[3] The banks and many of the stores had closed their doors and it was becoming difficult to buy food.

On December 23rd, General MacArthur pulled the American troops out of Manila and moved them into the hills northwest of the city. On the 26th, MacArthur declared Manila an "Open City", meaning there would be no defense.[4] This didn't stop the Japanese from bombing and strafing the city before they entered. The locals obtained less and less factual information as the situation progressively worsened.

Shortly thereafter, Japanese soldiers entered Manila. One day Harry's father went to the store and didn't return for several hours. When he finally arrived home he told the family that Japanese soldiers confronted him and made him go with them to show the soldiers where other Americans lived. On January 3rd, 1942, four Japanese soldiers knocked on the front door. One, an officer, spoke good English. He was armed with a sword, while the other soldiers had rifles. The officer told the family they had 10 minutes to pack enough belongings for three days and they were to come with him and his men. Harry's mother told him there was no way they could be ready in just a few minutes and told him to come back in two hours. Surprisingly enough, the soldiers left.

Two hours later the soldiers returned. The Robinson family believed they would be returning in three days, so they packed just a few clothing and personal items.[5] The soldiers escorted them outside and ordered them to get into the back of a stake-bed truck. It happened that quickly. In two hours the family's assets, mementos, everything not carried with them, were gone forever. Similar events were occurring all around Manila as American civilians-men, women and children, were rounded up.[6]

Harry's future brother-in-law worked in the sporting goods section of a department store. The day after the first bombing he went to work and his supervisor, a Japanese national, took his car keys, his wallet and the keys to his apartment. The attitude was one of "Cooperate or you'll get hurt". In the years before the war there had been a major influx of Japanese nationals into Manila and the surrounding area. Incidents like this added to the confusion. The Japanese were taking over Manila. People didn't know what to expect or whom to trust.

The Japanese took the family to the Santo Tomas University campus, a Catholic university in Manila, which was now being used as a prison camp. The camp encompassed roughly 30 acres and there would eventually be nearly 4,000 prisoners in the camp. Almost all were civilians. An 8-foot concrete wall surrounded the university, with gates on all four sides.

To Harry, this was still an adventure. He had no expectations going into the camp, but believed he and his family would be there just a few days until this war situation was resolved. None of them had any inkling they would remain in this converted prison for the next three years.

In the camp the males were separated from the females. On arrival his mother and three sisters moved into a room on the second floor of a building. His father and oldest brother, who had polio, stayed on the ground floor of the same building. Harry and his younger brother went to the third floor. His living quarters would be the corner of what was once the anatomy/zoology lab.

Initially, their treatment wasn't bad. The Japanese guards were more inquisitive than mean. There were two daily roll calls and they were forced to bow before the guards, but this was bearable. Their treatment became harsher when different guards were brought in. As Harry described it, the days were "filled with boredom, enhanced by lack of hope". He settled into a routine of getting up in the morning and going to the bathroom, and then to roll call. After this, he stood in line for breakfast and this was how he began his day. Every day was the same.

Everyone had jobs in the camp. Harry worked in the annex kitchen for two hours each day. One of his assignments was picking insects out of the food that would be served later. Early in his imprisonment he attended daily makeshift classes for 1 ½ hours in one of the classrooms. The classes were soon discontinued. He was able to play basketball and softball occasionally to pass the time.

In the early days the food was more plentiful and of better quality. This changed as time wore on. The oatmeal they received in the early days was replaced by watered down rice. Everyone lost weight. Outside vendors were occasionally allowed to sell food in the camp, but this didn't last. By 1944 the death toll was rising in the camp due to the lack of food, poor nutrition and overall living conditions. A pushcart was used to remove the dead and it wasn't unusual to see someone pushing the cart down the street, bearing with a corpse. When the camp was finally liberated in 1945, Harry was 16 years old and weighed 90 pounds.

The American invasion of the Philippines began at Leyte Gulf on October 20, 1944. They landed on the main island of Luzon in January 1945. Liberation for the civilian prisoners came on February 3, 1945, during a daring raid by the American 1st Cavalry Division and the 44th Tank Battalion, supported by Marine Air Group 24, who provided close air support with their SBD dive bombers. This task force pushed far ahead of the American lines and crashed through the gates of the camp. Their sole purpose was to get to the prison and rescue the prisoners, out of fear the Japanese would kill them. There was still much fighting to be done in Manila after the liberation of the camp and the prisoners stayed inside the walls. The Japanese repeatedly shelled the camp, killing several of the freed prisoners and fierce battles raged just outside the gates.

The Americans drove the Japanese out of the city and regained control after bitter fighting in the streets. The Robinson family and other families anxiously awaited transportation to bring them to the U.S. After being freed, Harry and his brother tried get it to their apartment to see if any of their former belongings and possessions remained. The area was flattened by repeated Japanese shellings and bombings and they discovered nothing remained.[7]

The family came to the U.S. by ship, arriving in May 1945, with little more than the clothes they were wearing. They were assisted by the Red Cross, who found them housing in hotels. Harry spent the summer adjusting to his new freedom and the climate. At the end of summer he enrolled at Washington High

School in San Francisco. He
was given a little bit of
credit for "time served" and
entered school as a junior.
He was older than the other
juniors and his life experience had been much different. He didn't tell fellow
students about his past, of
living in a prison camp for
more than three years.

Harry attended U.C.
Berkeley after high school
and graduated with a B.S.
degree. During the time he
was in school he received

Harry Robinson-recent photo
(H. Robinson)

several draft notices, which he managed to have deferred until
after his college graduation. He was finally drafted in 1954 and
spent two years in the U.S. Army. He stayed in the San Francisco
Bay Area after his discharge from the military, working for three
years at the Solano County Health Department. After a brief stint
in the medical supply business, he established his own bacterio-
logical supply business in Concord, California. During this time
he also married his wife and raised five sons.

Harry's wife of 44 years died a few years ago. He continues to
work in the business he started 42 years ago and lives in Martinez, California.

Harry's parents never regained the comfortable financial sta-
tus they enjoyed in the Philippines, although they were grateful
for the assistance they received from the American Red Cross.
Harry's father did receive some assistance from U.S. Rubber and
continued employment with them after his return to the United
States.[8]

NOTES

1. An older sister was already married and living outside the home.

2. Robinson couldn't see these fires, but this information came from other official reports.

3. At one point the warehouse where Harry's father worked was bombed by the Japanese and Harry's father avoided injury by taking cover in a pile of tires.

4. Some sources say this occurred on 12/25/41.

5. Harry doesn't' remember the family packing food. He recalls his sister brought a coffee pot and he made a campfire their 2nd day of captivity so they could boil coffee grounds to make coffee.

6. Civilians from other Allied nations were also being detained.

7. The family photo included in this story is one of the few items remaining from their life before the war.

8. The author interviewed Harry Robinson on 8/12/08 in Walnut Creek, California. He also listened to a presentation in Concord, California on 7/17/08 where Harry described his experiences at Santo Tomas.

■ ■ ■ ■ ■ ■ ■ ■ ■ ■

Chapter 3

Sunday Memories

Many men in the Third Thursday Lunch Bunch have distinct memories of where they were, what they were doing and how they felt when they heard of the Pearl Harbor attack on December 7, 1941. They couldn't possibly have understood at the time how this one tragic event would have such a profound impact their lives and influence the world as they knew it. These are a few of those memories.

****

Herman Denny graduated from high school in Watsonville, California in 1940. After briefly studying at Salinas Junior College, the 19 year-old took a job with Bank of America as a bookkeeper in the Concord, California branch office. One Sunday morning he heard about a stage play in nearby Antioch and decided to go to the play. He turned on the radio in his '32 Ford coupe as he drove leisurely through the countryside to Antioch late that Sunday

Herman Denny 1943
(H. Denny)

morning. It was announced over the radio that the American fleet at Pearl Harbor, Hawaii was bombed that morning by the Japanese. He was shocked to hear the news.

Joe Guevara on scooter he fabricated on Okinawa 1945 (J. Guevera)

Joe Guevara was a 17 year-old high school senior in Antioch, California. His mother died when he was seven and his father spent a lot of time traveling with his job. Joe's sister and her five children lived in the family house in Antioch and Joe fended for himself most of the time, living in a small room in an outbuilding behind the house. On weekends and after school he helped support himself with three part-time jobs. He delivered newspapers, worked in a grocery story, and sold magazines. He had some free time on Sunday morning and turned on the Atwater Kent radio for some entertainment. He was upset and angry to hear the Japanese attacked Pearl Harbor.

Fonzie Parrish 1945 (F. Parrish)

Fonzie Parrish was a 15 year-old boy living in Sprague River, Oregon. He was born in Missouri, but lived on a farm during his boyhood years in northeastern Oklahoma. His family moved to Oregon in 1939 and lived in a small town in the middle of the Klamath Indian Reservation. He was playing basketball with Ronnie Wilson in Ronnie's backyard. Ronnie was a Piute Indian. One of Ronnie's sisters ran into the backyard and told the boys that Pearl Harbor was bombed. They wondered where Pearl Harbor was. Fonzie knew there would be a war, but at fifteen, was certain the war would be over long before it would affect him. The U.S. had already started drafting young men, so the war couldn't possibly last until he was 21, the draft age. There was fear in Oregon and at other places on the West Coast that the Japanese might invade.

Larry Posey 1943 (L. Posey)

Larry Posey heard the news in Window Rock, Arizona. The 27 year-old Creek Indian was working as a secretary to the superintendant of the Navajo Indian Reservation. Larry grew up on the family home-stead in Oklahoma. He later at-tended an Indian boarding school in Lawrence Kansas and learned business skills. He married a Sioux Indian woman and they moved to the Navajo Reservation, at Window Rock, where the tribal headquarters were located. That Sunday morning Larry heard the news of the bombing on his radio. He immediately went out into the court-yard to notify his neighbors. Within a short time, several of the young Navajo men enlisted.

Fourteen year-old Lou Satz was working at his new job in a Chinese restaurant in Chicago. Lou had recently recovered from a bout with scarlet fever. To celebrate, his father bought him a brand new Schwinn Admiral bicycle. It was the fancy model, maroon and cream in color, with hand brakes. It cost $29. Lou wanted to make some money, so he got himself a job at the local Chinese restaurant as a delivery boy, using his bicycle for deliveries. At 50 cents a day, plus tips, he could make some money at this job.

This was his first weekend at the new job. He worked Friday night and all day Saturday and Sunday, getting to work at 11:00 am. He had borrowed $2 from his father so he could buy a basket for the bike. It would make the deliveries much easier. Lou was the only Caucasian in the Chinese-owned restaurant.

Sgt. Lou Satz 1946
(L. Satz)

Lou waited for deliveries inside the restaurant. It was at the restaurant where he first heard the news of the bombing. Customers continued to come in that day and several asked if the restaurant was Chinese-owned or Japanese-owned before they made the decision to eat there. The owners were quiet, obviously concerned about the question being asked by these patrons. Many of the customers appeared to be shocked at hearing of the bombing. It was certainly the main topic of conversation.

Lou returned home after work that night to find his father furious. His father had been a Navy ensign in WWI. He recalled his father's anger at the American fleet being bombed and the comment he made, "We'll get those bastards." Lou asked his father what all this meant and his father answered "You have no idea how big this is." Lou lamented the war would be over before he could get into it. His father wasn't as certain about this.

****

28

Americans all around our country felt the shock of this catastrophic event. Their lives and the world would be forever changed. These men and boys were no exception.

Herman Denny-recent photo (Author's collection)

Herman Denny volunteered for the U.S. Navy. He was assigned as a radioman on a minesweeper (YMS), with the rank of radioman 2nd class. He served in the Southwest Pacific, primarily off the coast of New Guinea. Herman returned to the U.S. and was training to be an officer when the war ended. After his release from the Navy in 1946 he attended U.C. Berkeley and graduated in 1951 with an accounting degree. Herman married shortly after he received his discharge. He and his wife raised a son and a daughter. He worked as an accountant in the private sector briefly before pursuing a career as a field agent for the IRS. Herman retired from the IRS after 24 years of service. He and his wife live in Walnut Creek, California.[1]

Joe Guevara was drafted into the U.S. Army in March 1943. He was assigned to the motor pool of the 98th Anti-Aircraft Artillery Gun Battalion on the island of Okinawa and drove trucks and M-4 tracked vehicles. Joe returned home and was discharged in 1946. He married and went to work for U.S. Steel. He and his wife

Joe Guevara-recent photo (R. Slominski)

raised two daughters and Joe retired after 39 years of service. They live in Concord, California.[2]

Fonzie Parrish finished high school a year early. By this time the need for manpower was great and the draft age was lowered from 21 years of age to 18. He swore he didn't want to be in the infantry so he volunteered for the U.S. Naval Reserve, just before he turned 18, in 1944. He was called up ten days later. After training, he was assigned to a new U.S. Navy ship that was ready to be commissioned, the *USS Pine Island*, a seaplane tender. Fonzie was assigned as a mail clerk. His battle station was at a 20-millimeter anti-aircraft gun.

The *Pine Island* and its 1000-man crew were sent to Okinawa in mid-1945. Fonzie had several opportunities to man his gun and defend the ship against kamikaze attacks. The Air Wing to which the ship was assigned assumed reconnaissance and rescue duties. The ship was anchored in Chimu Wan Bay, away from the main fleet, where there was plenty of room for its sea planes to take off and land.

Mail Clerk 2nd Class Fonzie Parrish returned to the U.S. early in 1946 and was discharged in July. He came to the San Francisco Bay Area to pursue his boyhood dream of managing and owning movie theaters. He retired from that career in 1970 and pursued a

second career as an insurance agent and broker.
Fonzie, now retired, has
two children and he and
his wife live in Walnut
Creek.[3]

Soon after the war
started, Larry Posey was
given another job. He was
put in the uncomfortable
position of working for
the War Relocation Au-
thority, commonly re-
ferred to as the WRA,
where he worked in the
accounting department.
This was the agency re-
sponsible for relocating

Fonzie Parrish-recent photo
(Author's collection)

Japanese-Americans from the West Coast to internment camps.
He described this as a sad experience.

Larry was initially deferred from military service because his
wife was disabled. Later the needs of the military increased and
he lost his deferment. In November 1943 he was drafted into the
U.S. Army. He heard that for some reason the airborne needed
men to train to be railroad engineers. This, coupled with the extra
$50 per month he would get for jumping out of airplanes,
sounded appealing so he volunteered to become a paratrooper.
The paratroopers needed medics more than train engineers, so
he trained to be a medic.

Posey was assigned to the 515th Regiment of the 13th Airborne
Division and sent to France in February 1945. He held the rank of
Technician 3rd Grade, which is equivalent to a technical sergeant.
On three separate occasions his regiment was slated to jump into
enemy territory. In each instance the American forces were

Larry Posey-recent photo
(R. Slominski)

Lou Satz-recent photo
(R. Slominski)

moving so quickly that the mission was cancelled. He never got into combat and thanks General Patton for his decisive moves and the fast-moving American forces.

The division returned to the U.S. in the summer of 1945. Larry's wife died at a young age, leaving him with a young son. He was a widower for several years and then married Rose, a Lakota Sioux Indian, in 1954. Together they have a son. Larry went to work as a civilian employee for the Army Transport Service in 1948. He was the dispersing officer on several ships and worked in this capacity for 17 years, until retirement. Larry and his wife live in Walnut Creek.[4]

Lou Satz was called into the U.S. Army in the summer of 1945 after finishing one year of college. He served with the Army of Occupation in Austria. You will read more about him later.[5]

NOTES

1. The author interviewed Herman Denny for this story in Walnut Creek, California on 4/7/10.

2. The author interviewed Joe Guevara and his wife, Joyce for this story in Concord, California on 4/12/10.

3. The author interviewed Fonzie Parrish for this story in Walnut Creek, California on 3/10/10.

4. The author interviewed Larry Posey for this story in Walnut Creek, California on 3/1/10

5. The author interviewed Lou Satz for this story in Concord, California on 3/13/04 and 3/14/04, during the making of the film *lives beyond the war* and spoke to him again on 4/28/10. The rest of Lou's story is told in Chapter 22.

Chapter 4

In the Hands of the SS

Ray Slominski was far from his home in Ardoch, North Dakota. After graduating from high school in 1938 he worked on his father's farm for a year and then joined the Civilian Conservation Corps and worked for two years with them. He worked for a few months at a tool company in Chicago and was inducted into the Army in October 1941. He was trained as a B-17 ball turret gunner and flight engineer and soon found himself at an air base in Bassingbourne, England with the 401st Squadron of the 91st Bomb Group. The 91st was one of the first American heavy bomb groups in England assigned to daylight bombing raids, in 1942.

The accommodations at Bassingbourne were considered 1st class by Ray's standards. This was a permanent base and their

Ray Slominski in basic training
1942 (R. Slominski)

barracks were 2-story buildings. The enlisted men from the nine crews in his squadron lived in one building and the officers lived in another. His group received a lot of publicity after their arrival in England and Ray thought one of the main reasons was the good accommodations for the news media when they visited, unlike some of the other bases. One of these crews in his squadron that received a lot of publicity was the crew of the *Memphis Belle*. Ray knew these men from flying training missions with them before going overseas.[1]

In the early days of the war there were no long-range American fighters that could defend the bombers on their missions. British Spitfires could escort them across the English Channel, but their limited range prohibited them from continuing deep into France. Ray arrived in England in October 1942 and flew his first combat mission on November 8th. He later joked it wasn't true what people heard about the bombers being unescorted. He said the British Spitfires took them across the Channel and the German Messerschmitts and Focke Wolfes "escorted" them to the target and back to the Channel. Here the Spits were waiting to take them back to England.

There was no shortage of German fighters and Ray experienced their attacks more than once on his first few missions. By the middle of December he had flown four combat missions, all of them along the French coastline. The weather had been bad and missions couldn't be flown for several days. The weather cleared for his fifth mission on December 20th and this was also his squadron's first mission inland. This would be his last mission. The target was part of a German airfield at Romilly-sur- Seine, where the ERLA company had a repair facility for Messershmitt fighters.[2]

Shortly after their British escorts left them along the French coastline, Focke-Wolfe 190 and Messerschmitt 109 fighter planes began attacking the group. As they flew inland the attacks became heavier and more intense. The German fighters came out of the sun, en masse, near Rouen. On the first pass the last plane was knocked out of the formation. Both pilots were killed and Ray watched below him as the plane went into a tight spin and spiraled downward, with the tail breaking off. He didn't think it was possible for anyone to get out, but one parachute came out of the tail.[3] Ray wasn't even sure where the initial attack came from, but the German planes that attacked were above him, out of his line of sight. Ray's plane was flying in the #2 position, on the right wing of the formation leader.

The second attack came just minutes later. The top turret gunner on Ray's plane, Allen Haynes, was hit by cannon fire from the attacking planes. The pilot, Robert English sent copilot Charles Mendel to check on the gunner. As Mendel went to Haynes' aid, the plane was hit in a second frontal attack. The pilot died instantly and slumped over the controls, sending the plane went into a dive, the #2 (left inboard) engine flaming. Mendel returned to the copilot's seat, struggling to pull the big bomber out of the dive.

Ray was in his turret and couldn't see what was happening in the cockpit.[4] He saw the engine on fire and the plane leveled out, after losing 5,000 feet of altitude. They were now alone, separated from the group while the German fighters continued their attack, making repeated passes at the stricken bomber. Ray heard Mendel give the order to bail out over the interphone. Stefula, the tail gunner, was severely wounded in one of the attacks. Ray positioned his turret with the guns pointing down so he could climb out the hatch and into the main fuselage of the bomber. He quickly donned his seat parachute, which he kept in the waist of the plane, made his way to the side exit door behind the waist gun position and pulled the release pin on the door. One of the other gunners kicked open the door and the radio operator, Jim Tyler, bailed out. The two waist gunners, Ralph Tomek and Vince Jakoby, followed. As Ray turned to face the door, German fighters made another pass at the damaged bomber and he was hit by machinegun or cannon fire in his left thigh and shrapnel from the exploding cannon shells peppered the right half of his body. It knocked him to his knees on the floor and felt as if he'd been stabbed with a hot poker in his thigh. Somehow he still managed to jump.

He immediately pulled the ripcord on his parachute and felt a jolt as the parachute opened. Then he lost consciousness. When he came to, he was lying in an open field. He felt excruciating pain in his left leg. When Ray looked down he saw a huge hole in his thigh, big enough to put his fist inside it. He sat up and when he did so, he lost his vision. When his vision cleared he saw a French farmer approaching. The farmer whispered "pistolet" in an urgent tone. The farmer wanted his gun. Ray didn't carry a gun and shook his head. He saw he was on the side of a hill, a plowed field. His leg was bleeding profusely now and he tried to get the farmer to understand he needed a tourniquet. It was no use. He couldn't make himself understood.

As this was happening two German soldiers approached, along with a group of French people. One of the soldiers cut off his parachute harness and the Germans fashioned a sling from the harness and parachute to carry him down the hill, where they had their car waiting. The soldiers lifted him into the backseat of the car. One of them drove while the other, in the front passenger seat, guarded him with a pistol. They took him into a nearby town and stopped alongside a row of buildings. Three additional soldiers came out of a building with a fourth, who served as an interpreter. The interpreter told Ray he had to ask some questions. Ray was in excruciating pain and told the interpreter he wouldn't answer any questions, so the soldiers took him to a first aid station of sorts. They carried him into a room and lifted him onto a table. He was wearing four pair of pants to protect him from the cold and the Germans cut all four pair off. Then the soldiers left.

Ray couldn't understand why they left. He faded in and out of consciousness. When he was conscious the pain was unbearable.

At one point a German soldier walked into the room and looked down at him. Ray focused on the soldier's face. The soldier saw the religious medallion Ray was wearing on a chain around his neck and removed it. The soldier read the medallion aloud, "Mary, mother of God, pray for us now and in the hour of our need." Then the soldier said to him, "Go ahead and pray and see if it does you any good." The soldier walked out. He knew he was in bad shape and thought he was going to die, but somehow wasn't bothered by the feeling. His final thought was of impending death as he faded again into unconsciousness.

Sometime later that night Ray woke up. He looked around and saw he was in a hospital room. [5] He couldn't move and realized he was in a body cast that went from his legs up to his chest. He felt around, checking to see that he still had all his body parts and heard a voice say "Hi, Ray". He looked across the room and saw Sal Dalterio, the tail gunner from the other plane that went down. He had never been so happy his entire life to hear another human voice.

Ray looked around and saw two German soldiers in the room. They were SS troops! He tried to move and couldn't move anything on the left side of his body, due to the cast. He recalled being surprised that the Germans felt they needed two SS troopers to guard him in his fragile condition. The German doctor entered the room, but didn't speak English. The hole in his leg was left unbandaged, but

Ray Slominski 1942 (R. Slominski)

there were several strips of tape across the wound. For the next few days the doctor would come and re-tape the wound, pulling it a little tighter each time in order to close the wound.

Ray didn't speak German, but came to the realization that this hospital had a lot of wounded German SS troops who were patients. A few days later, about 11 pm on Christmas Eve, some of the SS trooper patients came into his room and offered Ray and Sal hot wine they carried in pitchers. There were 15 or more, all in good spirits. Ray and Sal appreciated the offer, but both declined due to their condition. Just before midnight the soldiers turned off the lights, lit candles and placed them on a dressing table. Then, in unison, they stood at attention, faced the candles, raised their right hands in the Nazi salute, clicked their heels and said "Heil Hitler". It was spooky, downright spooky. After this they blew out the candles, turned on the lights and left.[6]

A few days after Christmas Ray was lying on a stretcher on the floor in the surgery room, where he was brought to have his dressing changed. A big SS trooper leaned over, looked him in the eyes and said, in excellent English, "I suppose you thought we were going to slit your throat when we brought you here. Ray answered, "I never gave it a thought." He never made a truer statement, since he was unconscious when he was brought to the hospital, but the comment stuck with him. His friend Sal was transferred elsewhere a few days later.

Ray had been in the hospital for two weeks when attendants came into his room after dark and lifted him onto a stretcher. They took him to the local train station and carried him to a platform. About midnight they loaded his stretcher onto a train, along with a group of wounded German soldiers. He had no idea where he was going, but Ray had a feeling it would be a long time before he tasted freedom again. He was right.[7]

NOTES

1. Ray commented during the interview that the *Memphis Belle* crew was a good crew, much like the men on his own crew, with one major difference. They made it home and Ray's crew didn't.

2. This information is from Luftwaffe pilot Otto Stammberger to a nephew of one of the men on Slominski's crew, dated 1/2/99. Stammberger was apparently in one of the FW 190's that attacked the plane that day.

3. This plane was piloted by 1st Lt. Dan Corson, per MACR #5381.

4. He heard from other survivors what occurred in the cockpit. He also learned Mendel stayed with the plane, in an effort to save the lives of the crew. Of the 10-man crew, three of the men were killed (pilot Robert English, top turret gunner Allen Haynes, and tail gunner Steve Stefula. The other seven men survived as POWs, although all were wounded.

5. He later learned he was in a hospital in Evreux, France.

6. I've been unable to confirm this was any sort of a common ritual. I contacted former Afrika Korps member Helmuth Orschiedt, familiar with the SS, who felt it was likely the troopers just had too much to drink and were trying to make an impression on the Americans. If this was their motive they were successful.

7. The primary sources for this story are a series of interviews with Ray Slominski. The author interviewed him during the making of the documentary *lives beyond the war* on 3/13/04 and 3/14/04 and also interviewed him again in Concord, California on 7/21/04.

Chapter 5

An Evening with Eleanor

I t was a delightful evening, simply delightful. George hadn't seen many women since he and the other men of the 32nd Infantry Division sailed from San Francisco in late April of 1942. Now it was the end of September 1943, nearly a year and a half later. After spending several months training in Australia, they had been fighting the Japanese in New Guinea ever since.[1] Now they were getting a brief respite. Here he was, enjoying fine dining with a very special American woman. She

George Fries on left, sharing a laugh with Eleanor Roosevelt
(G. Fries)

was much more attractive than depicted in the photos he'd seen and she was so nice and polite.

George Fries was a technical sergeant and Staff Aide to the division signal officer. He had been in combat since late 1942 and was relieved to finally get a break. Some of the men from his company, as well as frontline troops from other companies, were brought from New Guinea to Australia for an entire week. All the residents of Coolangatta were evacuated and the men got to spend a week relaxing.[2] The local women were also gone.

One of the first stops for many of the men was the one pub in town. The pub hours were very limited. It was open only from 10 am until noon and from 4 to 6 pm. These combat veterans quickly changed the rules, with a little show of force from a couple of the men who had pistols, and informed the owner his pub would now be open the entire time the men were there. After some discussion, the pub owner kept the pub open 24 hours a day during their brief stay.

There wasn't a whole lot for the men to do, but it was a welcome relief to be away from the snipers, air attacks, bugs and jungle. They could read, relax on the beach, or go to the pub. The houses where the local residents lived were all locked up and the men slept in tents or on the porches of the homes. George slept on a porch. It wasn't the Taj Mahal, but it was peaceful and they were right on the beach.

George had no idea why he was chosen for the honor, but some thought it was because he was normally polite and didn't use bad language. For whatever reason, he was selected to sit with Eleanor Roosevelt, the First Lady, at a special dinner. The men were surprised that someone so important was visiting them. No one important ever visited them in New Guinea. They heard of movie stars and other popular figures visiting other places, but New Guinea wasn't on the tour list. It was almost like they didn't exist.

Mrs. Roosevelt wasn't in New Guinea, but she wanted to visit troops who had been there. More importantly, she asked to spend the evening with enlisted men, not officers. Rumor had it she wasn't a big fan of General Douglas "Dugout Doug" MacArthur. Neither were many of the men, so it should be an interesting evening.

It appeared there were going to be all sorts of additional benefits from her visit. The day before her arrival, basketball hoops, ping pong tables and tennis nets arrived. This was great! The men would now be able to get a little exercise and have some friendly competition while relaxing. Maybe they'd even get a decent meal for a change. The food wasn't that great for the local Aussies, but it would be nice if they could get some decent food. They were tired of mutton. Even when the cooks chopped it up and tried to make burgers out of it, one couldn't mistake the taste.

Some of the more sickly men weren't being allowed to attend the event.[3] They were kept in a nearby barracks for the evening. It wouldn't do well for the First Lady to see what combat had done to these men, so they would miss out.

When Mrs. Roosevelt arrived at the mess hall she was accompanied by an American officer and another woman, her personal attendant. That was all, no big entourage surrounding her. She had a delightful smile and was simply one of the sweetest and most gracious women he had ever met. When they sat down to eat, the other soldiers were somewhat bashful and weren't saying much. The men were overjoyed to see the food arrive, roast baron of beef, with delicious side dishes. Some of the GI's couldn't hold back and immediately started eating. They left the conversation to George. A cameraman who had been traveling with the 32nd Infantry Division, George Strock, seized the moment, taking several photos of George and the other men with Mrs. Roosevelt. One would appear in *LIFE Magazine* a week or two later, but Strock gave other similar photos to George as keepsakes.[4]

Just as the picture was being taken, George was telling Mrs. Roosevelt the men loved her for coming to visit and added she brought the best food they'd had in two years. He wanted her to understand this wasn't their normal fare of mutton burgers. Mrs. Roosevelt laughed and answered she understood completely and that they usually brought in the finest food for her wherever she traveled.

The remainder of the dinner was spent in relaxed conversation. She asked George if the men believed their supplies were adequate. He answered as honestly as he could, not going into great detail about the miserable conditions in New Guinea. He had to be a little careful how he answered these questions, considering there were a couple of officers standing behind him, listening to the conversation. It was a night he would never forget.

The next day the tennis equipment, ping pong tables and basketball hoops were gone. They were just props brought in by the public relations people and the men never got an opportunity to use them. George's parents, at home in Michigan, received a phone call from friends a week or two later, asking them if they saw the photo of their son in LIFE. They hadn't and were excited to see his smiling face in the magazine.[5]

After this brief respite it was back to New Guinea and the continuation of war. When their job was finished in New Guinea they moved up to the Philippines and continued to fight the Japanese. Early in 1945 George and 10 men from his unit were sent back to the U.S. They were mentally and physically exhausted. Before George left, his commander offered him a field commission and a rank of 1st lieutenant, skipping 2nd lieutenant. It was a great opportunity for advancement, but he was tired of the war and tired of the military. He felt he could take no more. The Army agreed and George and the 10 other men received honorable discharges after they returned home. He had bronze stars for participating in five separate campaigns and participated in numerous beach landings in New Guinea and the Philippines.

George returned to his home in Kalamazoo, Michigan. He was born in Quincy, Illinois, but moved to Kalamazoo with his parents, two brothers, and one sister during his high school years. George was drafted into the Army several months before the attack on Pearl Harbor. When he returned home he wasn't in good shape physically or mentally. Among other things he was still suffering from dengue fever.

George got to know a Catholic chaplain in New Guinea and, although he wasn't Catholic, they became friends. The chaplain was also from Kalamazoo and returned home several months before George. The chaplain, Father Whelan back in civilian life, heard George was home and told George he wanted to see him. Whelan was going to be at a parishioner's house and asked George to stop by. Father Whelan enjoyed having a drink and asked George to join him for a drink. Whelan filled two glasses half-full with the parishioner's whiskey and handed one of the glasses to George. George wasn't much of a drinker, but he was happy to be home and in good company, so he sipped the whiskey.

About this time a pretty young woman walked out of the kitchen. George was immediately smitten by her presence and remembered little else of his visit with Father Whelan that night. Her name was Virginia. He invited her to dinner that night, but she wasn't sure she wanted to go out with him. George invited her out to dinner later, but she said she was busy.

Meanwhile, George had purchased a brand new Plymouth automobile. This was October 1945. The war had been over since August and the first new automobiles, in very limited production numbers, were being made available. George was lucky enough to get the first one in Kalamazoo. George invited Virginia to a concert and she accepted. He arrived in his brand new car. Several months later George and Virginia were married.

George worked for the Post Office for a couple years after the war ended and then accepted a position with the Muscular

George Fries on right, greeting Eleanor Roosevelt
at Muscular Dystrophy Association banquet (G. Fries)

Dystrophy Association. He became the National Director of Field
Staff. He moved his family to New York for a year and then
moved to San Mateo, California, where he and Virginia raised
their two children. After retirement they moved to Walnut
Creek, where they live today.

George saw Eleanor again. Many years later the Muscular
Dystrophy Association was hosting a luncheon and awards ceremony at the Biltmore Hotel in New York City honoring more
than 1,000 volunteers. They needed a celebrity for the event and
George suggested they invite Mrs. Roosevelt, who lived in New
York City. The board asked how they could possibly get her to
come and George told them of his earlier dinner with her and offered to invite her. He sent her an invitation, along with a copy of
the LIFE magazine photo from 1943. Mrs. Roosevelt soon responded, saying she'd love to come. She remembered meeting
the young soldier and his friends. She had another luncheon engagement, but wanted to come to honor the volunteers. She

George Fries–recent photo
(Author's collection)

offered to arrange her own transportation, but George had a limo pick her up and bring her to the event.

Mrs. Roosevelt was just as gracious as at their first meeting. George couldn't have been prouder as he escorted her into the banquet room and introduced her to Virginia. To have these two special women together made for another wonderful memory.[6]

NOTES

1. At the end of World War II the 32nd Division had more days in combat than any other infantry division, a total of 654 days in combat. The division had been overseas 41 months.

2. Coolangatta is about 70 miles south of Brisbane, on the southeast coast of Australia.

3. One estimate indicated 8,000 of the 17,000 men in the division had malaria by the end of the Buna campaign in early 1943.

4. Strock was also a tent mate of Fries in New Guinea while on assignment there.

5. The photo and accompanying photo appeared in the 10/11/43 edition of LIFE.

6. The author heard George Fries speak of his wartime experiences at a veterans' luncheon in Concord, California on 2/18/10 and did a follow-up interview in Walnut Creek, California on 3/15/10.

Chapter 6

What in the World Am I Doing Here?

Many of us have asked this question, caught in the midst of an unfortunate or unpleasant situation. Our soldiers, sailors, marines and airmen who experienced combat in World War II may have asked the question more frequently. They had every good reason to want an answer for the question, although the answer wasn't always forthcoming. Sure, one could answer that it was for God and country, but that didn't keep the question from returning "the next time". It was often an expression of disbelief.

Warren Engstrom asked the question as he read a letter from a friend half a world away. Warren was just 18 years old, sitting in the jungle in New Guinea. Born in Berkeley, he grew up in nearby Montclair and was drafted at the end of his senior year of high school in June 1943. He would be given his diploma later.

It wasn't that he didn't want to join the army. Warren was a second generation, American and was patriotic, like most teenagers at the time. His father came from Sweden and made a comfortable life for Warren and his family. Warren was an ROTC cadet captain at University High School in Oakland and was anxious to join up. When he received notice to register for the Draft he went right down and signed up. He even asked them to take him right away. He didn't have long to wait. Two weeks later he was called up. His parents attended his high school graduation in his absence.

By November 1943, Warren was on a troop ship, headed for somewhere in the Pacific. Many of the men who trained with him were on the same ship, so he would be going into combat with some of his friends, or so he thought. He was trained to be a member of a gun crew in an anti-tank company. Several weeks later they landed at a replacement depot in Brisbane, Australia. Warren had become ill while on the ship and spent most of the trip overseas in the ship's sickbay. On arrival in Australia he was transferred to a field hospital where he spent two weeks recovering from a respiratory ailment. While Warren lingered in the hospital, his buddies were shipped out, assigned to the 7th Cavalry Division. They went to the Admiralty Islands. It was in the hospital that he first saw the effects of malaria on American GI's. Several of the men were stretched out on their beds, shaking uncontrollably, covered with several blankets. He was anxious to get out of that place.

When Warren recovered, he was put on a boat, destination New Guinea. He knew no one and would be joining the anti-tank company of the 128th Regiment, 32nd Infantry Division as a replacement. He landed at the divisional headquarters at Saidor. The headquarters was at a coconut plantation. With no instructions on how to use it, he was issued a hammock for his first night. He strung it between two palm trees and was careful to zip up the mosquito netting. All was well until he heard the unsynchronized sound of an aircraft engine. It was a Japanese "Betty" bomber, attacking the nearby fuel dump. Others around him must have thought it comical as he struggled to get out of the netting and hammock and get to the nearest cover.

It wasn't long before he had experienced combat, up close combat. Since there weren't any Japanese tanks to be found, Warren and his anti-tank company were assigned to guard the perimeter with their 37 mm cannons. There were normally four of the cannons in their company. They cut down coconut trees, using the logs to make improvised pillboxes for their guns. They used canister rounds in the guns, anti-personnel ammunition that broke up into small fragments when fired. The cannon itself weighed 912 pounds and they often pushed it up the narrow jungle trails, exhausting work in the hot, humid, bug-infested jungle. Wearing their canvas fatigues with rubber-soled canvas boots, canteen and helmet, they kept their pants tucked in their boots and their long sleeves buttoned to try to avoid as much as possible the bugs and mosquitoes. They carried little else, except for the guns they were issued and ammunition. Warren carried an M1 rifle.

There were no front lines. The enemy could be anywhere. Snipers often hid in trees, waiting for the Americans to pass before shooting men from behind. The nights were the worst. The Americans spent their nights in foxholes and slit trenches, waiting and trying to get a little sleep. The men usually dug two-man foxholes. The foxholes were close together, making it difficult for the Japanese to get

Warren Engstrom in Japan 1945
(W. Engstrom)

between them. The Japanese were known for their banzai-style night attacks, with fixed bayonets and yells. No prisoners were taken on either side. It was kill or be killed, with no quarter given on either side. He would personally experience these attacks twice while in New Guinea. The Japanese tried to infiltrate the American lines regularly.

One day Warren received a letter from his friend Elizabeth Sams, a former, well-meaning classmate from high school. The Japanese had just broken through the American lines and he and the men in his company were brought up as reinforcements to drive the Japanese back. He was sitting in the back of a 2 ½-ton truck. In front of him he saw a wounded soldier, his head bandaged, with blood streaming down in his face. He read the letter from Elizabeth, in which she talked of campus life, dating, and life in general. He asked himself "What in the world am I doing here? I don't belong here. I belong home with my friends." It wouldn't be the last time he'd ponder the question and have these thoughts.

While Elizabeth and some of his friends were enjoying campus life at U.C. Berkeley, he was in a stinking jungle, with men dying around him. He wasn't bitter or angry, but he realized how different his world was from the lives of his friends back home and just how much it had changed in less than a year. He was still 18 years old and didn't even need to shave yet, but he was right in the middle of this war. Sometimes he had difficulty believing it himself. This was a turning point for Warren. From then on, his objective was staying alive. He would do everything he could to be a survivor.

In April they invaded Atape, farther up the coastline in New Guinea on LSI's (Landing Ship Infantry). There was more tough fighting here. It was a fight to the death and many died. One morning after an attack, Warren looked over the top of his foxhole and saw a dead Japanese soldier directly in front of the hole, with a bullet through his forehead. Warren hadn't shot him, but

Japanese prisoner northern Luzon 1945 (W. Engstrom)

one of the guys in a nearby foxhole must have fired the round. The Americans didn't leave their foxholes at night. Whenever noises were heard, they were often accompanied by a shot aimed in the direction of the noise, so shots were commonplace.

There was no real rest for the men and they were exhausted all the time. The Japanese weren't the only enemy. Many had malaria, dengue fever, also called "breakbone fever" because all the bones and joints ached and felt like they were broken, as well as dysentery and other tropical diseases and infections. If they were so sick they couldn't function, they were sometimes sent down the trail to an aid station. At the aid station they might get a decent's nights sleep. That was about the best they could hope for. Warren contracted dengue fever and amoebic dysentery, but considers it a miracle he was never wounded.[1] Another hazard was booby traps. The GI's learned to never touch a dead body, Japanese or American, for fear the corpse was booby-trapped.

Their food was normally C rations or K rations, eaten cold and out of cans and boxes. Some of their canned food came from Australia. The powdered Nescafe packets in the ration packs were sometimes replaced with tea bags, often with an accompanying note from their Aussie friends, apologizing for the lack of available coffee.

Water is critical to survival. Whenever they secured an area, one of the first things done was to hang a big, waterproof canvas bag, called a Lister Bag, filled with water, from a tree. The water was treated with chlorine and chemicals to make it safe to drink. The men took Atabrine tablets that turned their skin yellow, but offered some protection from malaria.

There was still a lot of fighting to be done. After several more months in New Guinea, the 32nd Infantry Division moved up to the Philippines. He and his buddies weren't told where they were going until they were on a LST (Landing Ship Tank). They

Japanese prisoners northern Luzon 1945 (W. Engstrom)

landed on Leyte. From there they went to northern Luzon and the Villa Verde trail where the division suffered heavy losses, many from Japanese artillery and mortars. In the Philippines a few Japanese soldiers surrendered and were captured, but the fighting was still fierce. They were still in the Philippines when the war ended in August 1945. General Yamashita, the Japanese commander, didn't surrender his troops until September 2nd.[2]

Several weeks after the war ended the 32nd Infantry Division landed in Japan at Sasebo Naval Base, on Kyushu Island. From here they went to Honshu Island. The war was over, but now they were temporary peacekeepers. Here in Japan, the Japanese were very well-behaved and there were no problems. When Warren first landed at Sasebo the streets were bare. There was no one outside. As the division marched down the streets to the train station, the Japanese were all in their homes, apparently afraid or apprehensive about these Americans. The first to come out were the children. Gradually the adults joined them.

At the end of 1945 the 32nd Infantry Division was disbanded and Warren returned home. He was sent to Camp Beale in California. Warren went overseas as a private and returned to the U.S. a staff sergeant. He was 20 years old and had been overseas 26 months, in combat much of the time. He was still yellow from the Atabrine tablets and very thin as he stood in line in the mess hall at Camp Beale, getting Army food for one of the last times before being released. The servers were German POWs, big healthy-looking survivors from the Afrika Corps, specimens of Hitler's "master race". Warren chuckled at what the Germans must have thought as he passed in line. They probably wondered how the Americans could possibly have won the war with these sickly-looking soldiers like himself.

Warren was discharged in January 1946 and returned to civilian life, readjusting to the life he left behind. He attended the U.C. Berkeley using the GI Bill and graduated with a degree in Economics in 1950. Warren married his wife, Shirley, in 1953 and

Warren Engstrom-recent photo (R. Slominski)

they raised three children. Warren was in the insurance business for more than 30 years in the Bay Area. He and his wife live in Moraga, California.[3]

NOTES

1. Dysentery continued to be a problem for him after he returned home.
2. Yamashita was tried as a war criminal, convicted, and hanged in February 1946.
3. The author interviewed Warren on 8/11/08 in Moraga, California and followed up with a phone interview on 4/18/10.

Chapter 7

Night Attack on Japan

Bob McKay was in his second year of college at North Dakota State in Grand Forks in February, 1942 when the Army Air Corps recruiter paid a visit. The Army was looking for volunteers to be navigators and bombardiers. The recruiter even hinted they needed navigators for a new plane that was coming out. This looked like a good opportunity for him, so he signed up. He finished the term and received his notice to report in October.

Bob was born in 1921 on a farm a few miles west of Benson, Minnesota. His father had a disabling injury from World War I and farming became physically too much for him. The family moved closer to town when Bob was six and that's where he and his younger sister grew up. It was a tough life for the family. While attending high school he worked with a survey crew during the summers and became interested in civil engineering. His boss suggested he consider going to college at North Dakota State and he enrolled there after graduating from high school.

After being sent to Santa Ana, California for induction, Bob was commissioned a 2nd lieutenant upon completion of bombardier training in Roswell, New Mexico. After a short leave he went to Hondo, Texas for navigation training and then was sent to

Bob McKay 1945 (B. McKay)

Great Bend, Kansas. There he joined the 444th Bomb Group that was being formed and was assigned to the 677th Bomb Squadron for combat crew training. It was there he learned his plane would be a new heavy bomber, the B-29 Superfortress. He had never seen a B-29 or a photo of one. He knew only that it was a new aircraft that was suppose to be secret and one of the test planes had crashed, which wasn't a particularly comforting thought.

The men didn't see a B-29 for a while because there weren't any at the base so they began their crew training in B-17's. It was a couple of months later that the first B-29 Superfortress arrived. It was a big plane, much bigger than the B-17's and much faster, with an 11-man crew. The first one was painted olive drab. It was in great demand and all the crews wanted a chance to fly in it.

Bob and his crew finally got their opportunity. He was most impressed with the fact that the new airplane was pressurized. This meant he and the crew wouldn't have to wear oxygen masks at high altitude nor all of the heavy flying gear they wore while flying the B-17. It was also a lot roomier. Bob's station was behind the pilots and there was room for him to stand up and even walk around a bit. He felt good about the plane.

Soon other B-29's began to arrive. These were all natural metal finish (silver), unlike the earlier plane, because it had been determined the paint decreased the airspeed. Now there were more

Bob McKay's crew in training 1944 McKay is standing, far right
(B. McKay)

opportunities for crews to train together. By April of 1944 the group was ready for combat.

Certain crews were assigned a B-29 to fly overseas. Bob's crew was assigned the original, olive drab plane, the only one in the squadron. They didn't take the entire crew with them. The gunners and bombardier were replaced by non-flying squadron officers. The men who were bumped would travel by ATS (Army Transport Service) and would go overseas by ship.

They carried a spare engine in one of the bomb bays and the other contained additional fuel tanks filled with gasoline. Bob didn't know their final destination, but knew they were headed for combat.[1]

The first leg of their journey took them to Bangor, Maine for refueling and then on to Gander, Newfoundland. While plotting their route, he began to wonder if their final destination was England. At Gander the crew was told they were going to India. The next stops were at Marrakech, Cairo, and on to their final

Early B-29's (58th BW)

destination, a temporary base at Charra, India. The conditions were primitive at Charra, but this would be their home for a while.

By now it was mid-April. When they were settled, the crews flew several supply missions, flying fuel, bombs and other supplies over the Himalayas or "The Hump" as it was known, to bases in China. The staging area in China for future combat missions was at Kwanghan, 1200 miles from Charra and supplies had to be delivered and stored there for the combat missions.

By this time some of the problems with these early models of the B-29 were becoming apparent. Several planes crashed on take-off and crews were lost due to mechanical and electrical problems. The B-29's had been rushed into production and the crews paid the price. The problems were identified and the remaining planes were modified.

Some of the crews flew their first mission to a railroad yard in Bangkok, Thailand. It was the next mission that drew everyone's attention. This was a strike against Japan itself. It would be the first raid on the Japanese home islands since the Doolittle raid in April

1942 and all the flight crews wanted to be on this one. Bob's pilot, Tom Welch, managed to get his crew assigned to the mission.

This was going to be a night mission. The crew flew from Charra to the staging base at Kwanghan, China. The planes were loaded with 500 lb. bombs and fuel. The crews attended a briefing in the mess hall/briefing hut, a thatched roof building.[2] They learned their target was the Yawata Iron and Steel Works on Kyushu Island. This was one of the main producers of steel in Japan, therefore an important target. After the main briefing the navigators from the 11 crews assigned to the mission had their own briefing, where they discussed the route, weather condi-

HELLON WINGS, Mckay's assigned aircraft late in the war. Note McKay's nickname "Stretch" beneath navigator's window (B. McKay)

tions and other information that would aid them in getting to the target and back.

The Welch crew took off late in the afternoon, alone. Although eleven planes were participating in this raid, they would fly individually to the target and back. The crews were excited about this one, the opportunity to finally strike back at the Japanese in their own backyard, but first they had to fly across

Japanese-held China and, within an hour after take-off, they were flying over enemy territory.

It was nearly 1600 miles to the target, so the trip was long, but uneventful. There was cloud cover when they left the Chinese coastline late in the evening. Their assigned bombing altitude was 18,000 feet. As they approached the target, flak started bursting around them. It was heavy, but not very close and caused no damage. The bombardier saw a break in the clouds in the target area and dropped the bomb load. They couldn't see if they hit the target, but they turned and started their long trip home in the wee hours of the morning.[3]

The pilots decreased their altitude on the way back to base and stayed between 8,000 and 10,000 feet. All was quiet until they were over the Chinese mainland, flying inland. Whoom! It happened so suddenly, there was no time to react. Bob was sitting at his navigation table without his seatbelt when there was a sudden thrust and the next moment his head hit the ceiling of the aircraft. They had flown into a thunderhead and hit a downdraft. They lost several thousand feet in altitude in the blink of an eye and the pilot struggled to recover control of the aircraft. Fortunately their speed was sufficient so that the big plane caught an updraft and the pilot regained control.

Bob was never so frightened in his entire life and this wasn't even associated with combat. The entire crew was wide awake and alert after this incident and they landed several hours later in Kwanghan, 13 hours and 40 minutes after taking off on the mission.

The crew was tired, relieved to be on the ground, and proud to have participated in this bombing raid. These bombs were a message to the Japanese. The message was clear and simple. "We can reach you now and this is just the beginning." The mission was a real morale booster for the group and the message was delivered over and over again as the crews bombed other targets in Japan.

There would be many other long missions for Bob McKay and his crew. They moved from their temporary base at Charra to a more permanent field at Dudkhundi, India after the Yawata mission. In the early months of 1945 they moved to Tinian Island in the Mariannas and continued their missions against Japan. Bob finished his 35 missions and had been promoted to captain. He was on his way home for a 30-day leave, on a stopover in

Bob Mckay-recent photo
(Author's collection)

the Hawaiian Islands, when the atomic bombs were dropped on Hiroshima and Nagasaki. The war was finally over.

Bob was discharged in December 1945, but remained in the Air Force Reserve. In 1947 he went to work for the Bureau of Indian Affairs (BIA) in Alaska. He married Helen, a Minnesota girl in 1949 and they raised four children. In 1953 he went to work for Standard Oil Company (now Chevron) in Seattle. While in Seattle, Bob would fly on weekends while in the Air Force Reserve, where he attained the rank of major. He was transferred to Chevron's Concord, California business office in 1971. Bob retired in 1983 from Chevron. He and his wife, Helen, live in Concord.[4]

NOTES

1. McKay later assumed the pilots knew they were going to India, but had orders not to tell the crew.

2. McKay didn't recall how many bombs were carried by each plane, but believed it was a reduced bomb load, due to the distance traveled, and the need to carry more fuel.

3. The mission report indicated good bombing results.

4. The author interviewed Bob McKay for this story on 4/10/10 in Concord, California

■ ■ ■ ■ ■ ■ ■ ■ ■

Chapter 8

A "Bastard Battalion" Tanker at Normandy

J ohn Ezersky and his friends in the 747th Tank Battalion sat off the coast of Normandy on June 6th waiting to get ashore. It would be another day until they landed on Omaha Beach. The New York native was one of two men assigned to drive a 6x6 truck filled with 5-gallon cans of gasoline. Each M-4 Sherman tank in his unit had two trucks assigned to it. One truck supplied fuel and the other was an ammunition truck. John had the rank of Tech 4 (Technician 4th Grade-equivalent to a ser-geant).

They boarded their LCT (Landing Craft Tank), manned by a British crew, on June 4th at Plymouth, England for a trip across the English Channel. They left port but soon returned, learning later the invasion had been delayed. They were provided little in-formation and they just had to wait for any news. They set off again on June 6th and were anchored off Omaha Beach later that day. This time the invasion was under way and John knew he was headed for combat. The skies above the invasion fleet were filled with hundreds of planes, American planes. Now it was a

John Ezersky at Rhine River
early 1945 (J. Ezersky)

matter of waiting in line to go ashore. They spent a restless night on the boat and their time finally came on the morning of June 7th.

As they approached the beach, John saw bodies of American soldiers floating in the surf. Wrecked landing craft littered the beach, many sitting at odd angles at water's edge. It was not a pretty sight. American dead were lined against the cliffs, waiting for identification and burial. There was a nearby aid station treating the wounded. There was shouting and yelling, a sense of urgency, as the tanks, ammo trucks and gasoline trucks were off-loaded as quickly as possible into the shallow water. There was no gunfire in their immediate area, although there was heavy fighting nearby as the Americans fought to hold their ground and advance inland. John and his partner, Sam Immelman, drove off the ramp, into the shallow water and up onto the beach. He looked toward the cliffs and saw the combat engineers had already done a good job of cutting out roads up the bluffs so vehicles could make their way off the beach and up to higher ground. A route marked by green flags showed the path off the beach.

A young Ranger lieutenant stopped their truck. He said he needed their truck to bring supplies to his men. John told him they had other orders. A major from the 747th intervened and asked the lieutenant what he needed. The lieutenant said he needed a truck temporarily to deliver supplies to his men. The captain gave John the permission and the lieutenant and two of his men piled the nearby boxes of supplies into the truck on top of the 5-gallon cans of gasoline. The lieutenant and his men led the way to the far end of the beach. They quickly unloaded the boxes and Ezersky drove his truck back to their starting point, finding the markers and drove off the beach, where he located his battalion.[1]

John found his unit bivouacked less than ½ mile inland from the beach. This would be where they would spend their first night in France. The commander ordered them to start digging foxholes. They were in a farmer's open field. John and Immelman decided it would be more comfortable to sleep in the truck than in a hole in the ground, so they ignored the order. Late that night the Germans shelled the field. They both took off running across the field, intent on reaching the closest tank, where they could seek shelter beneath the armored vehicle. The tank commander nearly shot them as they ran through the darkness, but they learned a lesson that night. In the future they dug foxholes if they were going to be outside at night and did as instructed, at least most of the time.

The 747th Tank Battalion was not assigned to an Armored Division. These divisions and their tanks spearheaded most of the advances across Europe. Instead, the 747th was assigned to various infantry units that followed behind the Armored Divisions and cleared out enemy pockets of resistance. On Omaha Beach and for the next few months they were assigned to the 29th Infantry Division. None of the units, armored or otherwise, had pushed very far inland, having met fierce resistance. Since the 747th wasn't assigned permanently to any division the men sometimes referred to themselves and other similar battalions as "Bastard Battalions".

It wasn't long before the 747th was engaged in heavy combat. On June 8th, a tank was lost outside of La Cambe. That same day six more tanks were hit and disabled by German 88 mm cannon fire as they supported the 29th Infantry in driving the Germans out of St. Germain du Pert. It was here John saw one of his own tanks destroyed and witnessed the horror of a tank crewman burned to death when he couldn't escape from the tank.

They were in hedgerow country, large fields and orchards surrounded by thick, impenetrable hedges called bocages, perfect places for the enemy to hide and fight. It was difficult to know where the front lines were located. Sometimes the Germans weren't in front of them, but alongside them or even behind them. In the thick hedges they couldn't be seen.

John's role was to keep the tanks supplied with gasoline. Whenever the tanks were low on fuel, he took his truck to the tank, where he and Immelman helped the tank crew by unloading the cans of fuel and passing them to the men, who filled the tanks. When his cans were empty he headed to the nearest fuel dump for more gas.

The war really hit home to him a few days into the battle when they crossed a forested area and saw dead paratroopers hanging from trees, their parachutes caught in the branches. They had apparently been killed during the early morning hours of D-Day. There were many close calls, such as the day when a half-track driving down the road several yards in front of him hit a mine and blew up. A gasoline truck wasn't the safest vehicle to be driving in combat, but his luck held out.

John and Immelman carried M1 carbines in their truck. Some of the guys in the 29th liked the carbines and didn't have them, so John traded his carbine with one of the infantrymen for a .45 caliber semi-automatic pistol. It was a lot easier to carry. Fortunately, he never had to use it.

The 747th had a very difficult time getting the tanks through the hedgerows. Various innovations and modifications to the tanks were made to help get through the thick trees and brush. Some were more successful than others, but it still came down to tough fighting. The infantry called for the tanks for a variety of reasons. They were used when the infantry encountered pill-boxes, tanks and other armor or fortified positions, and were also used to clear out snipers. They finally made it through the hedge-rows, but there was still a lot of fighting to be done.

By December they had fought their way across France, into Belgium and then Holland. In Holland, John met some women who worked for the Red Cross. They handed out donuts to the men near Maastricht. John became friendly with these American women and agreed to meet them at the YMCA in town, a common place of relaxation for the GI's. It was a welcome break to go into town where John enjoyed relaxing and getting away from the Army life, if just to have a cup of coffee. He and some of his buddies from the 747th met the ladies and they were sitting at a table when the colonel walked in with one of the lieutenants. John didn't always follow the rules and just happened to be wearing his civilian shoes with his uniform, figuring he'd dress up a bit and be more comfortable for this special occasion. Big mistake!

The colonel saw his soldier, wearing his army uniform and civilian shoes and wasn't happy. Tech 4 John Ezersky became Private John Ezersky. They took away his "easy" job as gasoline truck driver and made him the assistant driver on an M-4 tank.

John felt his new job was actually safer than driving a truck filled with gasoline, but thought the demotion was a little heavy-handed.

John Ezersky late 40's (J. Ezersky)

John Ezersky-recent photo
(Author's collection)

His tank commander had already lost two tanks in battle and John promised to bring good luck to the 5-man crew. Luck held out and they made it through the remainder of the war safely, with no injuries to the crew. He received further in-field training in Belgium and was one of the crews chosen to ferry the 30th Infantry Division across the Rhine River in March 1945 in amphibious-tracked vehicles (Amtracs). He ended the war at the Elbe River in Germany. He returned home in December 1945 and became a civilian again.

John always enjoyed sports and was an excellent basketball player. After the war he played basketball professionally for six years, including one year with the Boston Celtics. The sport paid so poorly in those days that he couldn't support himself. Reluctantly, he made the decision to quit playing basketball and became a cab driver in New York City, where he could earn a decent living and worked there for 31 years. He moved to California in 1981, where he married his wife. Ezersky worked as a cab driver in San Francisco an additional 19 years. He and his wife are both retired and live in Walnut Creek, California.[2]

NOTES

1. Ezersky never learned what supplies were in the boxes. He also didn't know at the time that a primary reason for the markers was to keep the heavy vehicles away from areas that hadn't been cleared of mines.

2. The author interviewed John Ezersky on 3/9/10 in Walnut Creek, California with a follow-up phone interview on 3/12/10.

■ ■ ■ ■ ■ ■ ■ ■ ■ ■

Chapter 9

Just Another Forgotten Island

Many of the island invasions in the Pacific received little attention from the news media at the time and were quickly forgotten, except by those who were there or by those who lost loved ones. One of these islands was Angaur. It was just three miles long, barely a speck on the ocean, just six miles away from another small island, Peleliu. Both islands, part of the Palau island chain, would be the scenes of heavy fighting in September 1944. Both the Japanese and the Americans would suffer heavy losses.

For the 81st Infantry Division, the "Wildcats", Angaur would be their first combat. The leader of the weapons platoon of I Company, 3rd Battalion, 322nd Regiment was 2nd Lt. Al Groeper. Al was a San Francisco native and graduated from Poly High School in 1936. He went to work for American Tobacco Company after high school and married his wife Shirley in 1940, after dating her for four years. World War II came along and Groeper enlisted in the Army in 1942, volunteering for the infantry. He passed the preliminary tests to become an officer, attended OCS (Officer Candidate School) and was commissioned a 2nd lieutenant. After that he received additional specialized training.

The entire division would eventually be transferred to the Pacific, but Al was sent in advance to Hawaii to attend the Jungle Training Center. When he finished the course he remained at the school as an instructor until his unit caught up with him. The entire division attended the Jungle Training Center. After this additional training, the division boarded troopships without being told of their destination. A day out to sea, they were given their orders, the invasion of Angaur Island, in conjunction with the 1st Marine Division's landing on nearby Peleliu.

Al Groeper at Guadalcanal 1945
(A. Groeper)

While enroute to Angaur they stopped off at Guadalcanal for a practice invasion. Here the first three waves of the invasion force boarded LST's (Landing Ship Tanks), while the remainder of the division boarded troop transports. Now they were headed for combat.

The 322nd Regiment, Al Groeper's unit, was landing on the northeast side of the island code-named "Beach Red", while the 321st Regiment landed simultaneously on the southeast side of the island, code-named "Beach Blue". The beaches were narrow, so it was imperative that the men advance off the beaches as quickly as possible. The job of the weapons platoon was to support the three rifle platoons in his company. For this task they had two .30 caliber air-cooled machineguns and three 60 mm mortars. Al and the 36 men in his platoon were apprehensive, but ready for whatever lay ahead. Al was provided with maps and other details when they left Hawaii and he had gone over everything with his men. During the several day trip from Guadalcanal to Angaur there was more time to prepare his men, but much of what they were to face was unknown.

The softening up process preceded the invasion. The battleship *Tennessee* pounded the island with its heavy guns, assisted by the guns of four cruisers. The aircraft carrier *Wasp* supplied dive-bombers that bombed the beaches. On September 17, 1944, inside the LST's the men boarded amphibious tracked vehicles. When the men were ready the clamshell doors on the bows of the LST's swung open and the tracked vehicles were launched into the sea, with a sailor at the helm in the front of the vehicle.

The vehicles began circling, waiting for the order for the invasion to start. Smaller ships were now firing rockets at the beach. When the order came, the first wave headed for shore, followed a few minutes later by the second. Soon it was time for Al's group in the third wave.

The fire wasn't as intense as expected, but the vehicles and men were taking sniper fire as they reached the beach. The men had piled boxes of provisions on the sides of the vehicle and when they felt the track on their vehicle touch solid ground, they immediately pushed the boxes off the sides into the shallow surf and sandy beach, to be picked up later by others. The men quickly exited the door on the back of the vehicle. The navy driver (helmsman) of their vehicle was later killed by a sniper's bullet. [1]

The beach was crowded and was only about 20 feet deep, leading into thick, thorny underbrush. Al urged his men to get off the beach and they moved into the dense vegetation. The men of I Company pushed forward, ever so slowly in the rough terrain, taking casualties from sniper fire, mortar fire and machinegun nests as they advanced. None of Al's men were hit, but the men in the three rifle platoons leading the way weren't as lucky. The weapons platoon mortars were of little use to the men leading the way because they couldn't be fired through the thick canopy overhead. At the end of the day the exhausted men dug foxholes for protection for the night. That night the Japanese attacked at different points along the American line of defense, but were repulsed.

On the second day the men continued their advance, yard by yard, with Al's weapons platoon supporting the rifle platoons with machineguns when requested. They were pushing toward the high ground in the center of the island where the Japanese had dug in. The rifle platoons were still taking casualties from sniper fire and an occasional machinegun or mortar. The Navy provided close-air support for the men on the ground. The Japanese snipers concealed themselves in trees, caves and crevices. It was hard fighting, some of it hand-to-hand and it would be another day until they reached the open plain toward the center of the island.

The men improvised. The men quickly realized the tripods on the machineguns were useless in this terrain. They removed the tripods and carried them like rifles, wrapping belted ammunition around the barrel as a stock to keep them from burning their hands, and fired the guns from the hip. Al had a pair of binoculars, but they were at a premium. He broke his binoculars in half, turning the lenses into "spyglasses", one of which he gave to his sergeant. They made do with what they had.

The men dug slit trenches and foxholes when they reached the plain. These would be their home for the next few weeks. During the daylight hours the company sent patrols onto into the hills on the northwest side of the island. This area was called Renauldo Hill, but it was actually a series of coral ridges. The Japanese had retreated to the ridges and were dug in. They weren't about to surrender, no matter what the odds, so it was a matter of finding them and killing them before they killed you or your buddy. It was a dirty business, but this was combat.

Late in the day the Americans came back onto the plain and returned to their foxholes, a safer place to spend the night. During the night the Japanese fired mortars at the American positions. The Americans were careful not to leave their foxholes at night and ordered to shoot any moving target. They took turns standing watch, an hour or two at a time. None of them slept well. For food the men had C rations and K rations.

The losses were mounting in I Company. Within a few days the company commander had been killed, as was the leader of the 1st platoon. By the end of the first week, of the 185 men in I Company that landed on the beach, only 86 were left who hadn't been killed, wounded or injured. Al's platoon had just a few losses, from sniper and mortar fire. The assistant company commander was wounded and the leaders of the 2nd and 3rd platoons were injured or wounded. Al was called in to take over leadership of the 1st platoon. Instead of providing fire support for these platoons he was now leading one.

He knew the men in 1st platoon, having trained with them. Still, he was a new leader. On the morning of his first assault up the hill he said "Let's go". No one moved and the men just looked at him. When Al started up the hill, they followed. He recalled it had been different in training. When he told the men to do something, they just did it. In training the Japanese weren't shooting at you. Perhaps that was the difference. This is where leadership counted.

Al carried an M1 carbine. That's what officers carried. The enlisted men carried M1 Garand rifles. The officers were also dressed differently wearing a 2-piece fatigue uniforms. The enlisted men wore one-piece fatigues. They wore no rank insignia, but the Japanese may have targeted the officers because of the difference in uniforms and weaponry.

Every day Al took his men up the hill, searching for the Japanese in their caves, crevices, and in the trees. It was a routine, a deadly routine.[2] The Japanese were quiet. There were no shouts of "Banzai!" or yells. The only noise heard was that of a sniper's bullet or an occasional burst of machinegun fire or mortar round. Later in the day the tired soldiers came back down the hill to their foxholes. At night Al took his turn at standing watch. He wouldn't ask his men to do anything he wouldn't do.

During the second week it happened. Al was on watch one night in his foxhole. Suddenly there were three mortar bursts just outside his foxhole. After the bursts hit he could barely hear. He wasn't wounded, but his hearing was severely impaired.[3] The next morning he went to the field hospital. Since he couldn't hear sufficiently, he was removed from combat. He stayed at the field hospital for several days and then was transferred by ship to a hospital at Guadalcanal. It took more than four weeks to clear the Japanese from the caves, holes, and crevices on the mountain at Angaur.[4]

After spending time in the hospital at Guadalcanal, Al recovered enough of his hearing to allow him to be discharged, but not enough to allow him to return to combat. He was sent to the 750th Port Battalion on the Russell Islands and was then transferred back to Guadalcanal with the battalion. Guadalcanal was a main transit base in the Pacific. Supplies from New Zealand, Australia and the U.S. were sent by ship to the island, then off-loaded and put onto other ships to be sent where needed. Al was made a stevedore officer in the battalion, which consisted of more than 200 officers and men, with the responsibility of directing the loading and unloading of ships. The battalion operated around the clock, in 8-hour shifts.

One night Al was having dinner in the Officers mess with a few of his buddies and had a few too many drinks. They were having stew again, a regular meal there. He had seen sides of beef being unloaded from the ships, good American beef, but the good cuts, like steaks, never made it to the men. He commented, "Who's responsible for this sh__?" He didn't notice the colonel behind him. The colonel growled "Groeper, I want to see you in the morning!" The next morning he reported to the colonel's office as ordered and was asked to explain the comment. Al explained he had seen there was good meat coming onto the island, but they never saw any of it. As a result of his explanation the colonel promptly made him the new mess officer.

Al Groeper-recent photo (Author's collection)

Al took his responsibility seriously. One of the first things he did was put a lock on the meat locker. The good cuts of beef were now under lock and key and no beef would be disappearing after it reached his kitchen. It wouldn't be just the cooks who enjoyed the steaks. He also made other changes. He acquired a butcher to cut the meat properly and acquisitioned an oven for baking. The men were accustomed to getting scrambled powdered eggs. Even when real eggs were available, the cooks scrambled them. The eggs weren't plentiful, but Al arranged it so the men could occasionally have eggs fried to order. The cooks and kitchen staff resented him at the beginning, but they fell into line when they saw the men were happier with the food.

Al was still at Guadalcanal when the war ended in August 1945. He and his battalion were sent to New Caledonia in

December. Al had enough points to return to the U.S. in March 1946 and he was discharged within a week of returning home.

He had several jobs during the first few years after the war ended, all in the San Francisco Bay Area, eventually becoming a salesman and manager for a life insurance company. During this time he also joined the California National Guard, eventually achieving the rank of major and the position of Assistant Divisional Signal Officer in the 39th Infantry Division. He resigned his commission in the mid-1950's due to family and business commitments. He and his wife raised one daughter. Al retired in 2003 after 50 years in the life insurance business. He and his wife have been married for 70 years and live in Walnut Creek, California.[5]

NOTES

1. Al didn't witness this himself, but heard about it from others.

2. He referred to this "routine" as a "mundane war".

3. Since he shed no blood, he did not receive the Purple Heart medal. This was classified as an injury, not a wound.

4. Losses were much higher on nearby Peleliu, where elements of the 81st Infantry Division had joined the Marines in battle.

5. The author interviewed Al Groeper on 2/16/10 and on 4/10/10 in Walnut Creek.

■ ■ ■ ■ ■ ■ ■ ■ ■

Chapter 10

The Watch

The story you are about to read was told at one of the group lunch meetings in 2003. On this occasion, there was no planned guest speaker and the group of men was casually visiting among themselves while eating their lunch. It was one of the smaller meetings, with about 25 in attendance. One of the men suggested that it might be nice if each person shared a short story and that is how this story surfaced.

Several stories were humorous, such as the story by the former fighter pilot about having a first date with a woman whom he met shortly before going overseas. The man arrived at her door and was shocked to see the young woman open the door wearing a wedding dress. He turned and ran across the lawn and down the sidewalk as she yelled behind him, "Don't leave! It's OK; I'm not getting married until tomorrow night!" Laughter filled the room as the men pictured the dashing young pilot tripping over himself in his haste to get out of there.[1]

Soon it was Bob Tharratt's turn to share a story. Bob, one of the group's founders, was a ball turret gunner in the 338th Bomb Squadron, 96th Bomb Group during the war, serving in the 8th Air Force in England. He began his story by talking about the

Bob Tharratt 1943
(B. Tharratt)

concepts of luck among the bomber crewmen and said many of the men were superstitious. Heads of some of the other former airmen in the room nodded in agreement. Bob recalled that many of the men were avid churchgoers, even those who had never been inside a church before going overseas. Others performed some ritual before going on a combat mission, while yet others carried good luck charms. Again several of the men nodded knowingly, in support of Bob's comments, for they had witnessed similar events. As Bob continued his story it became clear this was going to be a story about luck in wartime Europe.

Bob said a young B-17 gunner finished his training and was preparing to go overseas. The airman visited his family before leaving for Europe. While at home he received a gift from his father, who had been an aerial observer/gunner in a British Royal Flying Corps bomber during World War I, drawing aerial maps over France. The gift his father bestowed upon him was a watch. The father told his son the wristwatch had been a gift to him and he wore it on all his flights and credited the watch with getting him through the war safely. The father asked the son to wear the watch and told him it would help keep him safe. The dutiful son agreed.

The airman went overseas with his crew to the war-torn, dangerous skies over Europe. He shared the story of his father's watch with his crew and the crew decided to adopt the watch as a mascot, of sorts. It became their good luck charm. Before each mission the crew assembled by the plane. On the navigator's signal the entire crew set their watches with his watch. At this time the crew made sure that the airman had his watch with him.

The crew grew to believe in the luck of the watch as they were initiated into combat and began flying combat missions. Although other planes around them were shot down, they returned. While other planes in their formation returned with wounded or dead crewmen, not one member of this crew received a severe wound. On mission after mission they returned safely, during 17 missions, from targets like Munich, Regensburg and Schweinfurt.

The men grew to trust in each other as they gained combat experience. They also trusted in "their watch". As they prepared for their 18th mission, the crew gathered alongside their B-17. The navigator called for the crew to set their watches with his watch. The gunner raised his sleeve and the lucky watch wasn't there! He had forgotten it! Some of the crew told the gunner to return quickly to his quarters and get the watch, but the pilot stopped him, explaining there wasn't time. There were angry comments from some of the men as the crew crawled into to their bomber and made last-minute preparations for the mission ahead. The gunner knew some of the men weren't happy with him that day and the fact that he forgot something they believed was so important to their survival.

It was not a lucky day for the crew. While over Nuremberg that day in September 1944 their B-17 was hit by anti-aircraft fire and the crew was forced to bail out. The entire crew was captured and the men were put in various POW camps. Fortunately, all survived the war.

One of the men on a different crew was a friend of the airman with the watch. He was on the mission and saw the ill-fated B-17 go down. After returning from the mission, the friend went to the airman's sleeping quarters and, knowing the story of the watch, took it for safekeeping. This man completed his required number

Bob Tharratt's crew in the summer of 1944.
Bob is kneeling, far right, front row (B. Tharratt)

of missions safely and returned to the U.S., bringing the watch with him. He used a portion of his leave to travel halfway across the country to return the watch to his buddy's parents, who were extremely grateful to receive it.

As Bob neared the end of his interesting story, the others in the room were intently listening. One man whispered that he really enjoyed the story, but remarked that these fascinating stories were always about someone who knew someone else and most of the time couldn't be substantiated, although there was usually an element of truth in them. Bob continued with his story and, as if reading the minds of some of those present, remarked that these stories often couldn't be confirmed. As heads nodded again he took off the precious, lucky wristwatch that his father gave him and passed it around the room for everyone to admire. He finished by telling everyone he knew this story was true, because it was his story and his watch.

As the watch was passed among the men, they carefully held it and examined it, realizing the precious value of the watch, perhaps symbolic of time itself. Bob's watch is a reminder of the stories of these special men, stories that need to be told before their time runs out.

After Bob was shot down, he was sent to Stalag Luft IV in Poland. In February 1945 Bob and thousands of fellow prisoners left the prison camp on a forced march. They were told it would last three days, but 86 days later they were finally rescued by members of the 104th Infantry Division, known as the "Timberwolves".[2] He had survived this march of 500+ miles, with inadequate food and clothing, often sleeping on the frozen ground, during the coldest European winter in modern history. The march has become known as The Black March.

Bob was born in England and moved first to Canada, then to Cleveland, Ohio as a child, finally settling in southern California, with his parents and four sisters. After the war he briefly attended the University of California at Davis. After that he had a long career in the sales of concrete and concrete products and retired in Walnut Creek, California with his wife Jeane, after raising two daughters and two sons, where he lives today.[3]

Bob Tharratt and Ray Slominski (R. Slominski)

NOTES

1. That dashing young pilot was Frank Timmers, whose story is included in another chapter of this book.

2. Chapter 15 is a story about one of the "Timberwolves", Lou Boswell. Boswell was not one of Bob's liberators and was hospitalized at the time Bob was liberated.

3. Most of the information for this story came from a 2003 luncheon meeting. The author also interviewed Bob Tharratt again on 1/15/04, 1/17/04 and 3/31/10 as well as during the filming of *lives beyond the war*. Some of the background history came from Bob's book *I want you for the U.S. Army*.

Chapter 11

"Boys, We've Just Been Captured"

It came as a pleasant, unexpected surprise for Bill Armstrong and his buddy Bob Zellmer. It certainly showed that Lt. Ernest Allen was a good leader and a fine officer. Allen did his best to take care of the men in his command. Allen was the ammunition officer for Service Battery, 263rd Field Artillery Battalion, 26th Infantry Division. Bill and Bob were ammo truck drivers in Service Battery.

The 26th Infantry Division arrived in France in early September 1944 and saw their first major combat in October. Shortly after their arrival, Bill and Zellmer were called upon to teach the non-drivers to drive the Battery's trucks for what would be called "The Red Ball Express", keeping the front lines supplied with necessary supplies. Some of these American boys didn't even know how to drive a car, but most were quick learners and could manage the 2 ½ ton behemoths with the minimal four hours training provided.

Bill wasn't training drivers now. He and his buddy were assigned to supply ammo to "A" Battery, a group of four 105 MM howitzers and their 7-man crews. Initially they would bring a load of ammo to the gun, drop it off and drive back to Service Battery, until the guns moved or more ammo was needed. Now they stayed with the gun. When they saw the supply was getting low they drove to the ammo storage area, several miles behind the front lines, loaded the truck with boxes of the shells and returned to the battery.

Bill Armstrong in Austria 1946
(B. Armstrong)

This worked out well for the battery, but it wasn't that great for the drivers. The men at the firing batteries received hot food regularly. They had their own cooks to prepare their meals. Since the drivers weren't part of the battery, they didn't fit in the "Table of Organization" and had to scrounge for their own food. This meant they usually ate cold "K" rations or "C" rations out of a cardboard box. Their gourmet meal for this evening would likely be Spam from a can about the size of a tuna can, with powdered lemonade, a few pieces of candy, and a few cigarettes. Their menu didn't vary much.

Bill Armstrong was far from his home in Berkeley, California. He was born in December 1922 in Modesto, California and within a few years the family moved to Berkeley. Bill had one younger sister and the family came upon some hard times when his father decided to leave in the middle of the Depression. They survived, but times were tough. When the war came along, Bill's mother arranged with the family doctor to have him classified as 4F, meaning he had a physical disability that made him unfit for military service. He didn't approve of this, so he went down and enlisted in the Army in September 1942.

That all seemed like a long time ago as he and Bob sat in the cab of their 2 ½ ton truck, in a field near Arracourt, France. The guns hadn't fired for several hours now. Both wished this miserable rain would stop. It was November 6th and the weather had turned cold. It had been raining for days. Their clothes were damp and their G.I. shoes were caked with mud. The ground was so saturated with water that they frequently had to put chains on whenever they drove on unpaved roads, and then remove the chains when they were on pavement again.

Bill listened to the sound of raindrops hitting the metal roof of the truck's cab. There was still plenty of ammo at "A" Battery, so it would be a while before they would leave. He was starting to doze when there was a tap on the side window. Startled, he cranked down the window to see a shape in the darkness. It was Lt. Allen. Allen told them to get in his weapons carrier, that he was taking them back to Service Battery for a hot meal. They didn't need a second invitation! Bill and Bob grabbed their M1 carbines from the rack behind the seat, scrambled out of the truck and climbed over the tailgate and into the bed of the weapons carrier, which was about the size of a pick-up truck. The bed had a canvas cover and a flap covered the tailgate. Four other lucky truck drivers joined them. All of them had been with the guns for more than a week, so this hot meal would be a real treat. All six men were in a jovial mood as they set off on their journey.

Allen sat in the front seat of the truck alongside the driver, PFC Arno Melger. The trip would take a while, even though Service Battery was just a mile or two behind the lines. Blackout conditions existed in the war zone and the small lamps mounted on the front fenders provided little light to guide their way. They couldn't go more than 4 or 5 miles per hour, even in good weather and this wasn't good weather. Still, everyone was happy, looking forward to the hot meal.

The going was always difficult at night. The drivers some-times used a technique where they drove with one of the front wheels on the edge of a pavement, if the road was paved, so they could "feel" when the wheel ran off the road and make a correc-tion. In worse conditions one of the drivers would actually get out and walk in front of the truck down the center of the road, with his mess kit hung on the back of his web belt. The minimal light from the headlamps would reflect off the metal on the mess kit, helping the driver maintain a position on the road. Tonight Melger felt he was able to see enough to stay on the road without assistance.

After a few minutes, the truck suddenly stopped. Bill heard voices, GERMAN voices. He heard Melger, who spoke German, answer. This was not good. The flap on the back of the ammo car-rier lifted and there stood Lt. Allen. He said, "Boys, we've just been captured." Allen directed them to get out of the truck, slowly, one at a time, keeping their carbines pointed at the sky. When they were out of the truck, they were to release the ammo clip, then eject the live round from the chamber. Allen instructed them to lay the gun on the ground and put their hands up.

Bill recalls his first thought, even before he got out. He heard rumors about being captured and he thought, "Oh, hell! Now I'll be eating cabbage soup until the end of the war!" Armstrong was in the back of the ammo carrier and was first out. He did as in-structed. As he carefully climbed down from the truck, there was just enough light for him to see seven German soldiers with their rifles pointed at him. Their helmets were shiny in the rain. After he put his rifle on the pavement, he watched as the others fol-lowed. Lt. Allen and Melger were standing alongside him with their hands up.

One of the men in the back of the truck, Private Covell, was particularly jittery. He was always the nervous sort and now he was having a particularly tough time. He climbed out of the truck, with his carbine pointed up and ejected the clip. For some reason, probably out of nervousness, instead of ejecting the live round from the chamber, Covell pulled the trigger. BAM! The sound was loud and sharp. Bill swears to this day that he could see shiny pavement beneath the hobnail boots of the Germans as they jumped in the air. Melger shouted to the Germans, telling them in German that it was a mistake, imploring them not to shoot. There were some tense moments, but the Germans didn't shoot.

When the Americans were disarmed, standing with their arms in the air alongside the road, an amazing thing happened. The German soldiers turned their rifles around, handing them to the Americans, butt first. They took off their steel helmets, threw them to the side of the road and replaced them with their garrison caps. The Germans were surrendering! The first words uttered by the Germans was a request by one of the soldiers. "Kammerade, haben Sie zigaretten?" (Friend, do you have cigarettes?") Stunned silence followed as the G.I.'s struggled in their minds to process what had just occurred. One of the Americans laughed nervously and soon the entire group was laughing, Americans and Germans together. They were shaking hands, slapping each other on the back, and the Americans supplied their new German friends with the requested cigarettes. One explained to Melger that they knew the war was lost. They were sick of war and didn't want to die for a lost cause. The German soldiers were assigned to blow up a bridge on the road that night, but discussed it among themselves and decided to stop the next Americans they saw and surrender.

The Americans rearmed themselves and gathered the German weapons. They started walking, with Melger and Lt. Allen following in the truck. They had gone just a few hundred yards when they came upon the bridge the Germans were assigned to destroy. There was a .50 caliber machine-gun crew positioned on the road facing the direction they were coming from. The gunners had fallen asleep. Armstrong recalls feeling lucky the men were asleep and hadn't heard Covell's shot. This was a combat zone and there's a good chance the gunner would have started firing down the road. A .50 caliber bullet at 450 yards was deadly.

They crossed the bridge without further incident and, after walking for a while, Lt. Allen decided they didn't need so many men to guard the friendly prisoners. One man was left to escort the Germans to the prisoner detention compound, which was a large field surrounded by barbed wire and armed guards, and the rest climbed into the truck to return to Service Battery, still dreaming of that hot meal.

They had gone perhaps a mile when it felt as if they hit a brick wall. The truck stopped abruptly and Bill was slammed to the side of the truck. He felt blood streaming down his chin from a gash. Zellmer's cheek was slashed and the others had similar cuts and scrapes and were in a pile in the back of the truck. They exited the back of the ammo carrier for the second time that night to see what happened. In the dark, with little light coming from the headlights, Melger crashed into the back of another truck. It wasn't just a truck, but a truck loaded with German land mines recently removed from roads and fields by American engineers. The other driver, a black soldier in the quartermaster corps, was badly frightened and originally thought the mines had exploded.

After everyone calmed down, the men examined the vehicles, finding only minor damage, and they got back in the ammo carrier and continued on their way. On arrival at Service Battery a medic examined their injuries, which were minor. The medic told them they were eligible to receive the Purple Heart, for injuries sustained in a combat zone. The men all refused, knowing those medals should be saved for those who were truly wounded in combat. They were still looking forward to that hot meal, so after getting patched up, they made their way to the mess tent, only to find the evening meal had already been served. They found a cook who agreed to prepare a meal for them of........hot C rations.

The 26th Infantry Division was one of Patton's group sent into the Battle of the Bulge several weeks after this incident. They fought their way into Germany, and then moved southeast into Austria, finally finishing the war in Czechoslovakia. At war's end they moved back into Germany and became part of the Occupation Forces, charged with peacekeeping duties in Germany and Austria.

Bill was still in the 26th Infantry Division in August 1945, waiting for his points to catch up to him so he could return home. The military used a point system, a formula based on length of service, time overseas, medals, and other criteria. Bill didn't have quite enough points to return home, but knew he would be going home soon. Bill's life was changed that August in Ramshofen, Austria. It was here he met Vera Ivanovna Massuta, the love of his life. Vera had experienced the horrors of war. She was from the Ukraine, but was taken by the Germans as a forced laborer

B. Armstrong-recent photo (B. Armstrong)

when they overran her country. Now a displaced person, hundreds of miles from her homeland, her future was bleak.

The Cold War was beginning to take shape at the end of the war. Austria was divided into different zones. Vera was in the American zone when Bill met her. She was a world class athlete before the war, and the Russians knew she was in the American zone and wanted her back. The events that transpired as Bill hid her, protected her and married her would make a thrilling suspense novel, except the events are true.

Bill stayed in Austria when he was discharged in January 1946 and worked as a civilian employee for the U.S. government. He married Vera later that year and their first child, a son, was born there. Bill and Vera returned to the U.S. in 1947, where their daughter was born. Bill later went to work at the Concord, California Naval Weapons Station. He was a personnel development specialist and retired after 27 years of government service. Bill and Vera live in Walnut Creek, California. An ironic twist to this story is that he and Vera would never have met if he had accepted that Purple Heart medal. He would have had enough points to return home.[1]

(Author's note: See Bill Armstrong's story about crossing the Rhine River in Appendix B.)

NOTES

1. The author interviewed Bill Armstrong in Walnut Creek, California on 5/30/08 with a follow-up interview on 7/18/08. Bill also provided a brief written statement, summarizing the incident and the books he and his wife have written, *Dear Don: Letters to a Wartime Buddy* and *Bepa (Vera): An Autobiography* supplied helpful background information.

Chapter 12

Messerschmitt Attack

The weather had been simply terrible, with zero visibility, for several days just before Christmas 1944. At times there was two feet of snow on the ground. 1st Lt. Dick Bailey and the men of the 322nd Bomb Group, 9th Air Force, were frustrated and impatient for action. They flew the B-26 Marauder, a twin-engine medium bomber. Originally stationed in England and flying missions across the English Channel, the group moved to a base in Beauvais, France in September 1944 to occupy a former German fighter field they once bombed. The move brought them closer to the front lines and their medium-range aircraft could fly missions into Germany, if needed, as well as provide the necessary support for American ground units in France and Belgium.

This was a personal war. Most of their combat missions were in direct support of the infantry, the troops on the ground who were taking a beating in Belgium. Now the group was stuck on the ground. It was cold and muddy when the ground wasn't frozen. Their homes were tents, but the conditions were still much better than those troops in nearby Belgium. They heard the news about the big German breakthrough that occurred on

Dick Bailey in cockpit 1944 (D. Bailey)

December 16th in the Ardennes Forest. This breakthrough would later be commonly referred to as the Battle of the Bulge. They didn't have all the details, but they did know the situation was critical. The group managed to fly one mission on the 18th, in support of the 1st Army, but since then the weather kept them grounded.

Dick, a New York native, was a pilot in the 450th Squadron. He arrived in England at the beginning of the year and, after further training, was soon flying combat missions. Now, several months later, he was one of the more experienced pilots in his squadron, with 64 missions to his credit. He and his crew had lots of tales to tell of the missions, many in support of General Patton's 3rd Army after they moved their base to France. They didn't carry oxygen on their planes so their missions were typically flown at 10,000 feet or lower, well within reach of the German medium and large-caliber anti-aircraft guns. They survived many flak hits without injury to any of the crew. If he survived 65 he would get to return to the U.S. for a while, but that wasn't uppermost in his mind as he sat in the briefing room on the morning of December

23rd. The officers briefing started with the weather officer giving his report, telling the group the weather had cleared enough for a mission.[1] The weather was still not good, but finally they could get some planes up to support the troops on the ground.

The briefing officer revealed the target, a railroad bridge in Euskirchen, Germany, east of Aachen. Dick's crew and nine others from his squadron would join 23 other planes from the group in this effort. This bridge was on a vital route supplying the German troops with the materials to carry on their war in the Ardennes. It was also an escape route for the Germans. Its destruction would help the Allied war effort by stopping the rail traffic both in and out of the area. The crews were warned to be prepared for German fighter planes. Intelligence sources revealed the Germans brought up a lot of fighters in support of their attack in Belgium and it was likely they would be out in full force.

There was a sense of urgency as the briefing ended and the men prepared for the mission. Dick had a similar feeling on June 6th, as he prepared for his first of three missions he flew that day in support of the D-Day invasion. There was a brief stop in the equipment room where Bailey donned his back parachute, Mae West life preserver, flak suit and other gear. A truck picked his crew up outside and took them to their assigned plane. Bailey met with the crew chief and discussed the plane's condition. After a brief walk around the plane he climbed into the plane and prepared for take-off.

Dick's plane had a crew of six. In addition to the pilot and copilot, there was a bombardier or togglier[2], a top turret gunner/flight engineer, a waist gunner/radio operator and a tail gunner/armorer. The top turret gunner had two .50 caliber machineguns, as did the tail gunner. The waist gunner manned the single .50 caliber machinegun on each side of the plane, switching positions as necessary. In addition, there were four forward-firing .50 caliber guns, two mounted on each side of the plane, behind and below the cockpit. The guns were called "Package Guns" or "Blister Guns" by the airmen. These planes were originally intended to be used in low-level attacks and the purpose of the guns was to provide firepower for ground attacks. They had served no particular purpose for Bailey and he had never fired them.

The planes, with their engines running, waited for the flare, signaling the beginning of the mission. When Dick saw the flare, he began his taxi to the end of the runway, taking his position with the other planes in his flight. The planes quickly took off and assembled, flying one circle around the field at 2,000 feet. Dick's position was #3 in the flight of six planes, flying on the left wing of the formation leader. They headed across France and east into Germany, their airspeed registering 185 miles per hour as they approached the target in tight formation at 10,000 feet. They hadn't been attacked by fighters yet, and hadn't seen any, but they knew from the intelligence report they were in the area.

Their formation was tight as they approached the target, in order to get a concentrated bomb pattern on a small target. Bailey's wing overlapped the wing of the box leader. When over the

Dick Bailey's B-26 bomber *Pappy's Pram* 1944 (D. Bailey)

target they dropped their bombs and began a diving turn, still in tight formation, to pick up speed in order to get away from the target flak as quickly as possible. As they made their getaway with flak still bursting around them, the tail gunner called out over the interphone "Here they come!" Bailey looked up and saw tracer bullets over his canopy, stretching out in front of him. The Germans were attacking the group from behind! The fighters were even flying through their own flak, something he had never seen before. They must be desperate. Bailey heard the tail guns firing and then the top turret guns opened up. They were definitely under attack. Twelve to fifteen Messerschmitt 109 fighters were attacking the group from behind.

One of the fighters dived beneath them, a second climbed out above them and a third dived beneath them. They were so close when they passed that Bailey could hear the guns on the German planes firing. A fourth fighter closed in from behind, coming within yards of Dick's plane before he pulled up, the top turret gunner firing at him. Dick watched as the plane passed overhead and saw tracers from the top turret's guns stitch a pattern on the left side of the German plane from the cockpit forward to the engine. Black smoke belched from the engine and bright orange flames licked at the sides of the fighter as the top turret gunner's bullets stitched another row back from the engine and past the cockpit. The plane seemed to hang in mid air for what Bailey later described as "an eternity", and then the plane disappeared behind him. He heard the tail gunner shout over the interphone "He just exploded behind us!"

Other German fighters continued their attacks on the group, but none came as close as the first group. During the heat of battle a strange thing happened. The group was still in tight formation when a Messerschmitt 109 pulled up between Bailey's plane and the group leader. The German pilot was right under the flight leader's left wing, separated from Dick's plane and the flight leader by just a few feet. The bombardier in the plexiglass nose of the lead plane looked over in amazement at the German pilot. They were close enough that Dick could see the expression on his face. The German stayed in the same position for 20-30 seconds, looking side to side at both American planes. Dick could clearly see the pilot's unsmiling face, leather helmet and square goggles. Neither of the American planes could shoot, for fear of hitting the other American plane in the crossfire. The German dived away and out of sight. Was he taunting the Americans? Was he trying to make an impression on other German pilots? Only that pilot knows the answer.

Dick didn't' have time to question the German's motive. There were still other German fighters in the area and within seconds he saw one crossing in front of his plane, 200-300 yards away, crossing from left to right. Concerned now that the German might turn into them in a frontal attack, he decided to fire his "blister guns" at the fighter. He didn't even have a sight for these guns, but he wanted the German to see his tracers and hoped to scare him away. Dick slid his plane out of formation to the left, climbing several feet and pressed the firing button on the yoke with his left thumb. He saw the tracers arcing past the Messerschmitt and was surprised when he saw black smoke appear in the engine and the plane went into a dive, disappearing in the undercast. Dick slid back into the formation.

There were no more attacks on the planes in his formation. There were other air battles going on around them as P-51 Mustangs and P-38 Lightnings fought other Messerschmitts. Dick and his crew made it back safely, but some others in the group weren't so lucky. Two of the group's aircraft were shot down in the target area by fighters that day. A third badly-damaged aircraft made it back to friendly territory before the crew safely bailed out. In the returning aircraft four men were injured and one was killed. Dick's top turret gunner was given credit for destroying one Messerschmitt. Dick and his tail gunner were each credited with damaging a Messerschmitt. It was estimated that 50 or more German fighters attacked the group that day.

When the crews landed they headed to debriefing. Others in the formation confirmed Dick hit the Messerschmitt 109 and said it was last seen as it dived into the undercast, still smoking. The intelligence officer couldn't explain or even venture a guess as to why the Messerschmitt temporarily "joined" the flight. When discussing the fighter Dick hit, the people in Intelligence said they had never heard of another B-26 pilot in the ETO (European Theater of Operations) shooting down a German fighter. Reconnaissance photos later revealed the railroad bridge was still intact but both approaches were destroyed.[3]

When Dick Bailey returned to the U.S. in January 1945, he had been awarded two Distinguished Flying Crosses, 13 Air Medals, and five battle stars on his European Theater ribbon for participation in five separate campaigns. His group had also been awarded a Distinguished Unit Citation. He left the Air Force early in 1946 and returned to civilian life.

The Binghamton, New York native had enlisted in the Aviation Cadets in early 1942 and passed the exam to become a pilot. Now he was a civilian again. He considered returning to General Electric,

Dick Bailey-recent photo
(Author's collection)

where he worked before enlisting. General Electric was on strike so he made an important decision in his life, to return to school using the G.I. Bill. He enrolled at Rensselaer Polytechnic Institute in Troy, New York and studied engineering. He married in his senior year, obtaining a degree in mechanical engineering in 1950.

Dick worked for various companies in New York State, before being offered a position in California in the early 1960's. He and his wife raised four children. He is now retired and lives in Concord, California.[4] When recently asked how he felt about the mission on his return to base, he answered "We earned our pay that day." How true.

NOTES

1. The enlisted men attended a separate briefing.

2. A bombardier was an officer. A togglier was an enlisted man who had less training. Since most of the bombing done by the planes in the flight dropping their bombs as the lead plane dropped its bombs using the Norden bombsight, less training was needed and, theoretically, less rank.

3. This information, along with group loss details and German fighter claims are from the 322nd Bomb Group Unit History.

4. The author interviewed Dick Bailey for this story on 1/5/10 in Concord, California, with a follow-up phone interview on 3/7/10. He provided a story he had written for the book *The Annihilators, 322nd Bomb Group, Book 2*, and some of the details from this story were also used for background information.

Chapter 13

Long Night in the Ardennes

Martin Turkington had his 23rd birthday after his arrival in England by troopship in November 1944. A machine gunner in Company B, 289th Infantry Regiment, 75th Infantry Division, this was his first stop on his way to continental Europe. He didn't know his exact destination, but knew he was headed for combat.

Martin was born in Kansas City, Kansas, but traveled around a lot in his younger years, moving with his family to Oregon and then to Washington. Always independent, he left home in the middle of the night when he was a high school junior to work during the bee harvest and then went to work in a factory. He later hitchhiked to Kansas City, where he stayed with an aunt for several months and finished high school.

He tried to enlist in the navy in 1940, but was turned down because of poor eyesight. Martin registered for the draft and was drafted in 1942. The needs of the military changed dramatically after Pearl Harbor was bombed and his poor eyesight was no longer an issue. After several months of training and various assignments around the country, he was assigned as a machine gunner in the 75th Infantry Division. Earlier he was turned down when he requested a combat assignment, but now he would finally get his chance.

After spending a few weeks in Great Britain, his division boarded ships, destination somewhere in France. Heavy rains and rough seas tossed the ship as it crossed the North Sea and landed at Le Havre, France. From here they went to Yvetot, about 50 kilometers northeast of Le Havre, still far from the front lines. The men used their shelter halves for tents and set up camp in empty fields. The ground oozed mud from the heavy rains, making for cold, wet, miserable living conditions. It would get worse, much worse. The men patrolled the area, wading through the mud, waiting for further orders and assignment.

Martin Turkington 1945
(M. Turkington)

Rumors abounded regarding their future destination, but most thought they would be sent to the Hurtgen Forest, to reinforce troops battling there. On December 16th, while the division was still bivouacked at Yvetot, the Germans launched a counteroffensive in the Ardennes area of Belgium, a battle that would later become known as the Battle of the Bulge. The battle was in its early stages as Martin and the other soldiers in his division boarded boxcars, headed in the direction of Liege. It was on the train that he heard of the German breakthrough and learned their destination, the Ardennes Forest. On December 21st the division left the boxcars and boarded trucks for various assembly areas. They were now in a combat zone, although the lines weren't clear, due to fast-moving attacks by the German panzer divisions.

Turkington, or "Turk" as he was called by his friends, could hear the big guns firing in the distance. He and the rest of B Company were moved up to a line on December 27th. C Company had already been involved in a fire fight. The 289th Infantry Regiment was assigned to defend a line approximately five miles long between Grandmenil and Erezee, Belgium. There was a gap in the line between where C and A Companies had dug in and B Company would fill this gap.

It was rainy and cold as the 160 men of B Company marched through a pasture to a heavily wooded area. Late that afternoon they were ordered to stop and dig foxholes. They men removed their entrenching tools from their packs and started digging, intent on getting them as deep as possible while there was still daylight. The ground was full of tree roots and rocks, making the digging slow and tough. Turk was a member of a .30 caliber light, air-cooled machine gun squad. He was the gunner and the other members consisted of his squad leader, an assistant gunner and two ammo bearers. There was no room in the hole for the entire team, so the squad leader and the assistant gunner shared his hole. The three of them dug as quickly as possible, making the hole about 6 feet long and 30 inches wide. Darkness came quickly in the forest, but they continued digging, mounding the dirt in front of their foxhole to provide additional protection against a frontal attack.

On both sides, spaced several yards apart, other members of B Company were also digging. After dark the rain turned to snow as the temperature dipped below freezing. Turk and the others were freezing, but they could do nothing about it. They weren't dressed for this weather. Turk's clothes consisted of underwear, socks, wool shirt and pants, a fatigue jacket, shoes, leggings, a poncho and his helmet. His feet soon became numb from the cold.

Darkness prevented the men from seeing more than a few feet in front of them. There was no moon, but even if there had been, they wouldn't be able to see it through the heavy forest canopy of fir trees. They continued digging, piling the loose dirt in front of the hole, straining to watch and listen as they dug, chopped tree roots and removed rocks.

For several hours nothing happened. By 11:30 p.m. their hole was about 15 inches deep when Turk heard a sound off to one side. It sounded like footsteps on tree branches. The men stopped digging and stared into the darkness. Turk had placed his machinegun on the mound of dirt in front of him and now he aimed it in the direction of the sound. It was quiet again. The noise came just from a few feet in front of several foxholes down the line a few yards. Turk and the men in his foxhole had the machinegun and the men in the next three foxholes were armed with rifles. In the fourth foxhole, near the sound, was a friend of Turk's, armed with a B.A.R., a Browning Automatic Rifle, a one-man machinegun.

Turk looked through the black night and falling snow, but all he saw was darkness. Suddenly he heard a voice say, "Nicht schiessen" (don't shoot) and the soldier with the B.A.R. opened up. The muzzle flashes from the B.A.R. revealed five German soldiers at the front edge of the foxhole where the fire came from. Two German soldiers fell to the B.A.R. fire and Turk opened up and the other three Germans fell to his .30 caliber fire.

Suddenly it grew quiet again. The German patrol, searching for the American lines, had been stopped. Questions filled the minds of the men of B Company. There were more Germans out there, but how many? Would they attack in force? How near was the main force? If attacked, could they hold them back?

For nearly two hours it was quiet. The next attack came from in front of Turk. The German squad leaders opened up on the Americans with submachine guns, with their squads firing rifles as the Germans ran at the American positions. The flashes from the muzzles of the German guns were the first warning. Turk opened up with his machinegun, spraying bullets back and forth across his field of fire. His steady stream of fire stopped the attack and some of the Germans fell just a few feet in front of him. German machinegun fire now seemed to be concentrated on him, from both his left and right side in front of him and the tracer fire seemed to be aimed directly at him and his gun. The Germans were trying to get him in a crossfire. After several minutes the fire lessened and then stopped. It was going to be a long night.

Turk remained alert, peering into the darkness, trying to see in front of him He hoped the other men were as alert. He had the machinegun and could do the most damage in the attacks. The Germans knew this, so he and his gun would be their primary target. As Turk looked in front of him he saw sparks flying through the air in his direction and then saw the outline of the sparking object, a German hand grenade, as it landed with a dull thud in the dirt a few inches from his nose. He yelled "Duck!" and the men in the hole put their heads down just as the grenade exploded. The blast was so close it lifted the steel helmets of the men in the foxhole, jerking their chin straps against the undersides of their chins. Turk recovered quickly and moved his gun to the opposite side of a bush that blocked his view. A second grenade exploded in front of the hole. He struggled to see through the darkness and saw the outline of a human figure as it rose up on one knee, 12 or 13 feet in front of him and off to the side. Turk fired, his tracer bullets temporarily illuminating the area. The German soldier, positioning himself to throw another grenade, fell to the deadly fire.

Turk moved the gun again to face the direction of the main German threat. He didn't have long to wait. Submachine gun fire from another German attack raked the American lines as German soldiers charged. Turk fired again, pivoting his gun back and forth and more Germans fell. He began throwing grenades and yelled for others to give him their grenades if they weren't using them. At times during the night it looked like there were solid lines of tracers from both sides of the lines, much of it aimed at the main obstacle for the Germans in this area, Turk and his machinegun.

The squad leader, armed with an M1 rifle, was also busy firing, and the assistant gunner was shooting his .45 caliber semi-automatic pistol at the Germans and both men were also throwing grenades at the attackers.

The men repelled the second attack. The Germans then fired mortars and the Americans heard the "swoosh" sound of the mortars being fired in the distance in front of them, followed a few seconds later by the explosions close to the foxholes that lit the area for a split second. Someone on the American side called in artillery fire and shells burst ahead of them in the forest.

These Germans were fanatics and weren't backing off. They were even screaming during their attacks. One yelled "You die tonight Yankee." He heard another yell at the Americans, calling them "Rosenfeld's brothers", an anti-Semitic remark. These weren't just German Wehrmacht soldiers, but Nazis to the core. Throughout the night he heard German names being called in the darkness and thought perhaps it was one of the German officers or sergeants trying to account for his soldiers.

Turk's gun was so hot from continuous fire that the breech glowed red in the darkness, casting an eerie light in front of the foxhole. At one point the gun fired by itself, probably from the heat and twice during the night shells lodged in the gun and he had to quickly clear the jams in the darkness before he could fire again.

The third major attack came just before dawn. Once again the automatic fire was directed at him and his gun as the Germans charged the American lines. Turk answered the fire with his gun, mowing down more attackers. Many of the Germans fell within a few feet of the foxholes, but none of the charges reached the foxholes that night. By the early morning hours he recalls wondering just how much a man could endure.

When dawn fell the attacks stopped. The bodies of the dead German soldiers were strewn across the area and several were just a few feet in front of Turk's gun. The Silver Star citation, which he later received for his actions that night, said that 16 German soldiers were lying in front of his gun. He

Martin Turkington, taking a break in Germany April 1945
(M. Turkington)

didn't count them. Turk stayed in his foxhole until late morning, waiting for the next attack, which never came.

When he finally left his foxhole later in the day, he approached one of the dead Germans and saw twin lightning bolts on the collar of his uniform. He and his buddies, completely green troops who had never previously experienced combat, were sometimes referred to by some as the "The Diaper Division", due to their inexperience. Yet they had just repelled repeated attacks by elements of the 25th Panzer Grenadiers from Hitler's crack 12th SS Panzer Division. Turk searched the dead German for documents. While doing so, he removed a photo from the pocket of the man's tunic. The photo was that of a young, smiling woman, with two small children, on a front porch somewhere in Germany. It was a family photo. It must have been

Martin Turkington-recent photo
(B. Armstrong)

the soldier's wife and children. The dead soldier was wearing the Iron Cross medal.

Turk and his buddies stayed in position for two or three more days. There were no more attacks. The Germans retreated, although the Americans didn't know it at the time. As cold as it was, Turk was glad for the falling snow. It covered the bodies of the German soldiers.

This was only the first of several intense battles that Martin Turkington experienced as his unit advanced into Germany, but it was most certainly his longest night. He spent 27 days on the front lines before getting a temporary break from combat. He was a private first class when he arrived in Belgium, but advanced in rank to staff sergeant before the war ended five months later. He was wounded twice, but not seriously. His division had advanced deep into the Ruhr, the industrial region of Germany when the war ended in May.

Martin returned to the United States in November 1945 and was discharged a month later. After the war he went to radio school and became a radio electronics officer and began his career as a merchant seaman. He met his wife Florene, a nurse, aboard ship, and they married in 1949 and raised two sons. He retired in 1987 and lives in Martinez, California. He and his wife have been to Belgium several times, making friends there and retracing his route through that country. He still thinks of that German soldier and the photo occasionally. He doesn't dwell on it, but it's an image he can't forget, even after all these years.[1]

NOTES

1. The author interviewed Martin Turkington in Walnut Creek on 5/30/08 and interviewed him again in Martinez, California on 7/5/08.

Chapter 14

Operation NORDWIND Prisoner

He was surprised and confused. It was over that quickly. The 19 year-old infantry scout looked over at his buddy, Wallace Brown, in the slit trench alongside him. Neither of them was injured, at least not visibly. Tom Morgan looked up and saw Germans all around them, looking down and pointing their burp guns at him and Brown. It was January 2, 1945 just a little while after dawn. He had no idea there were that many Germans around.

Poor Brown. If this hadn't happened he would have been sent home. The 16 year-old Chippewa Indian from Minnesota was too young to be here in the first place. Brown's mother finally contacted the Army Adjutant and blew the whistle on the young enlistee. He was already told he was being sent home and would be on his way if this hadn't happened.

This most recent engagement started on New Year's Eve, but they had been engaged in combat since early November, when the 100th Division replaced the decimated 45th Infantry Division. After their training, they were sent overseas by ship, landing at Marseilles, France on October 20, 1944. Early in November, after

Tom Morgan 1944 (T. Morgan)

having spent several days in the port city, they went by truck convoy 400 miles to the front lines, near Rambervilliers, France.

Tom reflected on his arrival. The French army was also in the area. As he and the men in his unit surveyed the area when they first arrived, all was quiet. A ravine separated the Americans from the German forces, or so they were told. They couldn't see any sign of the enemy. A jeep filled with French soldiers drove up, with a machinegun mounted on the back. The French opened up with their machinegun, shooting across the ravine and beyond. Tom and his buddies had no idea at what they were shooting, since he couldn't see any evidence of the Germans in the distance, but Tom figured the experienced Frenchmen knew what they were doing. The jeep drove off as quickly as it came. They didn't have long to wait before they received a shelling from the German 88 mm guns. For whatever reasons, knowingly or unknowingly, the French had given away their positions. The Americans were mad as hornets at the Frenchmen.

This was their first taste of combat on their first day on the front lines. They were constantly on the move for the next two months, in pitched battles with German forces as the Americans advanced and the Germans retreated, with casualties inflicted on both sides. On a larger scale this advance would later be called the 7th Army's Winter Offensive. To the infantrymen on the ground it was more personal, towns and small villages to be taken at the cost of human life. These were places with strange-sounding names like Raon-l'Etape, Neuf Maisons, Salm, Baccarat, Saarburg, Lemberg, and Gotzenbruck. Tom was injured once when he was hit by a German bullet on his finger, the main force of the bullet being deflected by the trigger guard on his rifle. It was a minor injury and he remained with his unit, Company K of the 399th Infantry Regiment. They passed through what were once beautiful, thick forests in this mountainous terrain, now with trees sliced in half by artillery fire. It was such a waste, but this was war.

The weather turned cold and the ground was muddy and sloppy when it wasn't frozen. After they reached the front lines there was no more riding in vehicles. It was all walking. The wet conditions made it difficult to dig the foxholes to protect themselves during the night hours. Occasionally they came across abandoned French or German foxholes. They didn't have to dig as much when this happened, but it wasn't easy going. The men didn't get much sleep, as they shared guard duty, protecting their buddies, two hours on watch at a time. Most of their food came from boxes or cans. The one good meal they got was on Thanksgiving, when turkey with all the trimmings was brought to them. By then their stomachs were accustomed to the bland, packaged food and nearly the entire regiment suffered from diarrhea the next day. This wasn't a good thing in a combat zone. The men could laugh about it later, but it wasn't funny at the time. By the end of November the hard fighting in the Vosges Mountains was finished. They were now ready to advance into the Alsace region. It wouldn't get any easier.

There was continued heavy fighting as the Americans advanced in December and approached the town of Bitche and its fortress. They were at the Maginot Line with its series of WWI fortifications. Some of the battles in the villages were house-to-house. The Germans weren't retreating without a fight, but struggling to hold ground. By December 20th the pace had slowed dramatically. The Americans tested the defenses in the German fortress at Bitche by sending squads out to probe the defenses. The fortress was heavily defended and the Americans didn't get very far. As a scout, Tom was sometimes the lead man for his squad. The Battle of the Bulge was now raging to the north and the weather was getting progressively worse. The men of the 100th Infantry Division were digging into defensive positions. There had been snow earlier, but the first really heavy snowfall of the season fell on December 31st and at 5:00 pm the Germans began a major counterattack.

Multiple attacks occurred during the next day and a half, with large forces of German infantry assaulting the American positions along their line of defense. Several of the American positions were overrun and some of the American groups pulled back or retreated. There were dive-bombing attacks by German Stukas, as well as artillery and infantry attacks.[1] Tom and his squad weren't right on the front lines, but close, having been given a temporary break and they were being held in reserve. When the New Years Eve attack started, Tom saw a series of flares in the distance. This announced the attack. The men weren't aware of everything that was happening, but could hear rifle fire in the distance. This wasn't unusual, since their line of defense stretched for miles and there were frequent skirmishes along the lines.

During the night of January 1st, K Company started to pull back. A 12-man squad was brought up to the front lines just before dawn on the morning of January 2nd and left to guard the perimeter. Two of these men were Tom Morgan and Wallace Brown. They were told to man a slit trench. Their trench was 6 feet long and only 15 inches deep, not nearly as good as a foxhole, but they weren't given a choice. The other men in the squad had positions nearby. The rest of the company was pulling back.

They had been in their position for just a few minutes when the attack came from their right flank just after dawn. Brown and

Tom were both firing their M1 rifles at the enemy. As soon as they saw a head visible in the distance, they'd fire. Tom couldn't see if he hit anyone, but he kept firing. The other men in the squad were doing the same. Suddenly a grenade hit just outside their trench and exploded. When Tom regained his senses after the concussion he was looking up at Germans.

German hands grabbed the rifles from Tom and Brown and pulled them from the trench. He couldn't believe that many Germans were out there. Several of the others from the squad were also captured, while others managed to escape. Germans were all over the place.[2] There were even tanks coming up the road. The small perimeter guard was no match for this group. They marched the Americans to a nearby road where they were frisked. Tom had a German gun cleaning kit with him and a German soldier removed it. The soldier who removed it said "Deutsch?" Tom didn't answer. He thought this could be the end for him, if the Germans suspected he took it from a soldier he had killed, but nothing happened. There was no retaliation. They had him remove his socks, but allowed him to keep his shoes. They also took his watch. He, Brown and the others were marched to the fortress at Bitche, which was just a few hundred yards away. There a German tried to interview him, but Tom refused to give any information. The German didn't speak English and didn't continue the questioning.

The Germans put them in a cell for the night. The next day they began a two-day march, finally reaching a town with a rail yard. By this time there was a large group of captured Americans. It was a cold march, particularly so since the Germans had taken his good socks. Food was minimal, with just watery soup to eat along the way.

The situation got much worse when they were loaded into boxcars, the old French boxcars designed for 40 men or 8 horses. Sixty-five or seventy men were loaded into each car on the train, the wounded and bleeding as well as the able-bodied. The wounded needed to lie down, but some of the men had little consideration for them. There was no discipline, whatsoever, and no organization. Occasionally the men would call out "Pissen" or "Schissen" to let the Germans know they needed to use a toilet while the train was stopped or along a siding. As often as not, this was answered by rifle fire as the Germans shot up into the train from ground level outside the train. Fortunately, the German gunfire hit no one. Their destination was Stalag 5A in Ludwigsburg, Germany.

It took two full days to travel the 80 miles to Ludwigsburg. There were multiple stops and the train often stopped for hours at a time. They were given no food along the way and suffered through the freezing, crowded conditions. By the time they arrived Tom was violently ill, with stabbing pains in his chest. He was separated from Wallace Brown and the others and placed in the prison camp hospital or lazarette with eight French POWs and one Polish POW. It was definitely a prison setting, with guards and guard dogs patrolling.[3]

The men in his room were all diagnosed with tuberculosis and were isolated from other prisoners. He was fortunate there was an Army medic in the hospital helping the diseased and sick prisoners. There was little care available in this hospital, but the medic stood his ground to help the men. The medic insisted that Tom couldn't be moved when others were being marched out of the camp. Tom credits this medic, Masa Uchimura, with saving his life. He could never have withstood a lengthy march in the coldest winter in recent history. Uchimura was a Nisei (second generation Japanese-American) and a member of the highly-decorated 442nd Regimental Combat Team.

Sy Brenner, another army medic, witnessed the specifics of Uchimura's efforts that day and credits him with saving the lives of Tom and 18 other sick POWs who couldn't be moved. Two German soldiers came to where the sick men were being treated and isolated, intent on removing them to join the group of prisoners being gathered for the march. Brenner knew these men couldn't survive a march. He witnessed as Masa stood in the doorway of the room, with arms spread, barring the German soldiers from entering the room. Masa repeatedly told the Germans the men were sick and couldn't be moved, saying "Red Cross" and "Geneva Convention". The Germans, who didn't speak English, finally backed down and left.[4]

There was little food available in the hospital and what was there consisted of a grassy soup and black bread that tasted like sawdust. Not all survived. For some reason the French patients in the room wanted nothing to do with the Polish soldier, who was extremely sick. Tom befriended the soldier, who spoke no English and who couldn't communicate with him The Polish soldier's condition continued to weaken and he died in Tom's arms before they were liberated. Tom dropped from 145 to 95 pounds during his time in captivity. They were finally liberated by the French 1st Army at the end of April. By then most of the able-bodied prisoners had been moved from the prison camp and were taken on forced marches.

After liberation Tom spent a couple of days exploring nearby villages. He was soon flown to a hospital in Paris and then flown back to the U.S. for treatment. He went to various hospitals and was eventually diagnosed as having atypical pneumonia, not tuberculosis. After his recovery Tom returned to Oakland, California, his hometown. He had enlisted in the Army before he graduated from University High School in 1943 and was called up in December of that year. He was glad to be home again.

Tom enrolled at U.C. Berkeley, using the G.I. Bill to obtain a degree in Political Science. He married his wife in 1952 and later began a career in the insurance business. He moved up the ladder and at one point was a V.P. at an insurance brokerage in San Francisco. He and his wife moved to Walnut Creek, California in 1956, where they raised their son and daughter. Tom's wife died in 1994. He has since remarried and still lives in Walnut Creek.[5]

Tom Morgan (R. Slominski)

The German counterattack in which Tom was captured was code-named "Operation Nordwind". It was the last major offensive by the Germans on the Western Front, led by three divisions. Men like Tom Morgan of the 100th Infantry Division held off this attack.

NOTES

1. Tom did not see the dive-bombing attacks, but the information was recorded in the Unit History for the division. These attacks occurred miles away from his position.

2. The 399th Regimental Report revealed more than 100 Germans attacked this position.

3. Tom lost track of Brown, but records reveal he was released from Stalag 4B at Muhlberg at the end of the war.

4. The author spoke to Sy Brenner in a telephone conversation on 4/11/10 and learned the details of Masa's actions that day. Uchimura, now deceased, was recommended for a medal for his lifesaving efforts by Sy Brenner, but did has not received recognition. Brenner treated the wounded prisoners in the camp, while Masa treated the sick and diseased prisoners.

5. The author interviewed Tom Morgan for this story on 3/10/10 in Walnut Creek, California and did subsequent phones interviews on 3/14/10 and 3/24/10.

Chapter 15

They Did the Best They Could

Many of the vets who were interviewed for this book preferred to focus attention away from themselves. Several wanted to relate stories of their buddies, particularly in reference to combat situations and individual acts of bravery. The interview with Lou Boswell followed a similar course.

Lou is a practicing psychiatrist in Walnut Creek, California and my interview with him took place in his office. During my interviews I tried to keep the focus on the Vet and his personal story for the obvious reason that this book is about them. As I was setting up video recorder, Lou said he had to tell me a story about his brother. He said, "Turn on the recorder". With some apprehension I complied, and this is the story I heard.

Lou was born and raised in Cleveland, Ohio, with a sister and a younger brother. He was drafted into the U.S. Army and, after further training, was assigned to the 104th Infantry Division, known as the "Timberwolves", as a squad sergeant in a rifle platoon of "C" Company, 415th Regiment. His division was sent overseas by troop transport and arrived in early September 1944 in France. They were sent to the front lines in Belgium and soon engaged in combat near Brussels, then advanced into Holland.

Bob Boswell on left, Lou Boswell on right,
with their father in the center 1944
(L. Boswell)

When Lou was shipped overseas he was hoping his kid brother, Bob, wouldn't have to go. Bob was also drafted and plans were already set in motion to keep him out of combat. Bob was going to be assigned to the same division, the 104th. There was increased sensitivity in this country after it was widely publicized that the five Sullivan brothers from Waterloo, Iowa all perished when the ship on which they were serving together, the cruiser *USS Juneau*, was torpedoed in November 1942. Bob was not going to be in direct combat, but would be assigned to divisional headquarters, far behind the front lines and out of harm's way. These plans were set in place for this to happen.

Sometimes things don't go as planned. When Bob arrived in Europe, sometime after Lou, he was sent to a replacement depot. A jeep was assigned to take Bob to divisional headquarters, but an officer commandeered the jeep and Bob lost his transportation. Instead, Bob was put in a truck with other soldiers and taken to the front lines near Metz, France. He was assigned to Company C of the 1st Battalion, 2nd Infantry Regiment, 5th Infantry Division. It was not long before he was in combat on the front lines, wounded in the leg and hospitalized. When he recovered sufficiently he was sent back to the front lines.[1]

Lou had none of this information. He was fighting in Holland. He didn't know when Bob arrived, where he was assigned, or that he was wounded. He pieced the story together later, much later, after the war ended.

Near Bitburg, Germany Bob was in a 6x6 truck with his squad, returning to the front lines, when a German tank came out of a wooded area, blocking the road. The tank fired and the truck exploded, killing everyone in the truck, except Bob. He was badly wounded, unable to move, drifting in and out of consciousness. Shrapnel had torn his throat open and he had multiple other wounds, including serious injuries to his hand and shoulder.

A day and a half later the Americans had retaken the area, pushing the Germans back. Some soldiers from the Graves Registration Service were moving through the area, identifying, tagging and removing the bodies of the American soldiers killed in the recent fighting. They came upon the truck and the bodies strewn about. They found Bob and rolled him over. When they saw blood still flowing from his neck they realized he was alive. They left him lying on his back, taking his wallet. At some point after that medics found him and took him to a hospital.[2]

The family was frantic. They didn't know what happened to him. Bob was taken to a field hospital in Scotland, but the family was unaware of this. His injuries were so severe, particularly the throat and neck injuries, that the doctors could do nothing to help him or improve his condition. Lou was still unaware that any of this was happening.

Father Richard, an uncle of theirs, was a Jesuit priest. He was in Europe at the time, on official business with the Vatican, visiting various parishes. Lou's parents contacted Father Richard and asked him to help them. Father Richard finally located Bob in Scotland. Through his efforts arrangements were made for Bob to be flown back to the U.S. Father Richard left, believing Bob would soon be flown home. The family later learned Bob had been taken off the plane to make room for some officers returning home. When Father Richard learned of this he intervened again on behalf of the family and Bob was shipped to the U.S. on a Dutch steamer.

Bob was unable to eat while on the ship and there were no special provisions to treat him. A Dutch seaman assisted Bob on the 2-week crossing by feeding him liquids through a straw, directly into his throat.[3] Bob was taken to Walter Reed Hospital on his arrival. His mother met staff at the hospital and was told that little could be done for Bob's injuries. The wounds were simply too serious. Bob's father, a medical doctor himself and a World War I veteran, also came to the hospital. He told hospital officials he was going to stay there until they fixed Bob.

Bob had multiple surgeries over the next two years. His throat was so damaged that the best he could do was a raspy whisper. A failed surgery on his right hand left him with only a thumb and one finger and his left arm hung, nearly useless. Shrapnel in his head damaged the nerves and one of his eyelids drooped. Shrapnel wounds on his body left him badly scarred.

Lou stayed in Europe for several months after the war ended. He was in the hospital for a while, being treated for injuries and then worked with the army tracking down black marketers and assisted in obtaining restitution for French civilians. He returned home at the end of the year, arriving in the middle of the night. He had been told little or nothing about his brother's condition. By now Bob was strong enough to go home for the holidays.

Needless to say, Lou was shocked to see Bob for the first time. Lou hadn't seen him since before going overseas more than a year ago. He was also angry, particularly when he heard the circumstances surrounding what happened to Bob. Bob shouldn't have been in combat. Arrangements were made and assurances were given and this shouldn't have happened. There were major screw ups by a bunch of people. It made him sick.

A second shocking moment was seeing his mother. She was a commercial airline pilot, a real rarity in those days. When he left for overseas she was a strong, confident, vibrant woman. In less than two years she turned into a little old lady. This is what the stress of having two sons away at war had done to her.

Lou helped with his brother's rehabilitation after he returned home, while Bob was treated at the VA hospital in Cleveland. Lou also enrolled at Western Reserve University in Cleveland, ultimately obtaining his medical degree. Bob never gave up. A couple of

Lou Boswell in Eschweiler, Germany late 1944 (L. Boswell)

years later Bob also enrolled at Western Reserve. He graduated Phi Beta Cappa and went on to obtain his medical degree. Despite the huge physical challenges, which most would have found insurmountable, Bob went on to become an anesthesiologist and practiced for 45 years. Bob never gave up. He continued to have medical problems with his throat, which ultimately caused his death a few years ago, but he always had a good attitude and his great sense of humor carried him through the rough times. Still, this shouldn't have happened and he shouldn't have been in combat.

When Lou finished telling me about his brother, I asked him to tell me about being an infantryman in Europe and about the conditions. Lou described for me the terror of combat. His platoon of 40 or so men had more than a 200% casualty rate by the time the war ended. Not one of the original men in the platoon was still there and even the replacements were replaced.[4]

He described the chaos of having no officers to direct them because they were all killed or wounded, of having no medics much of the time because they were killed or wounded, of not knowing what happened to men in his own company, just knowing they were gone. His regimental commander was killed during the second day of combat. He lost most of his platoon in a battle one night near Aachen. He talked of the confusion, the mistakes made, of being bombed and shelled by his own troops, and the insanity of war.

Lou talked of the living conditions, never getting a furlough, of being frozen and not feeling his feet, of being ordered to keep their feet dry when it was impossible to do this standing in knee-deep water in their foxholes, with no replacement socks. They were constantly on the move and then there was the fatigue factor. It never ended.

Gunfire. There was always gunfire somewhere, behind them, alongside or in front of them. It wasn't always close, but it was always there, a constant reminder. He couldn't get away from it. He told of the one time when they got clean clothing. They put the clean clothes on right over their dirty clothes because they were freezing.

He recounted an episode of being at the front lines and someone sending a jeep to get him, being told the general wanted to see him. It didn't make sense to drive down the road. The supply sergeant was killed in a shelling while driving down that same road near Eschweiler, Germany. It was crazy to go down that road in the daytime, knowing the Germans had the road zeroed in. But orders were orders, so they drove down the road to meet General Allen, and fortunately weren't shot at or hit. The general presented Lou with the Silver Star.

He had no expectation of surviving the war, so medals didn't mean much. When the General gave Lou the medal, he told him to wear the medal not for himself, but for his men. Lou realized

General Allen was right. Every single one of these men who served with him was a hero. So many didn't survive.

There was no plan. It was just a matter of reacting. He knew it wouldn't stop until they got there, wherever "there" was. His single goal was to survive, but there was no expectation of survival. Ultimately, terror took over everything. It was pure luck that determined whether or not one survived.

Lou turned down a battlefield commission. He wanted no part of it. He wanted no responsibility. Besides, officers had even less chance of survival. Things were so insane that Lou and his platoon tried to stay ahead of their own lines, far enough ahead that neither the Germans nor the Americans would be shelling them. It's absurd, but they believed this was their best chance of survival. This concept was delusional, but it gave them something to believe in.

Lou was in the hospital recovering from a neck injury and trench foot when the war ended in Europe. He started out as a squad sergeant. He was more of a company sergeant at the end, although this wasn't an official designation. So many of them were gone and he took on whatever duty was necessary.

After Lou graduated from medical school in 1952 he practiced psychiatry in Ohio for a few years before moving to Nevada and then to California, ultimately settling in Walnut Creek, where he and his wife live today. Along the way he found time to raise eight children, four sons and four daughters.

Bob Boswell died three years ago of complications from his throat and esophagus injury that fateful day 63 years earlier. About two weeks before his death, Bob's wife phoned Lou and told him that Bob's condition was deteriorating. Lou talked to Bob on the phone and told him he must write his story of what happened to so someone can publish it and so people can understand what was going on, of how messed up things were for him, the whole story. He told Bob he owed it to everyone to tell the

Lou Boswell-recent photo (R. Slominski)

story. Bob responded, in his raspy, barely audible voice, "Lou, they did the best they could."[5]

Suddenly Lou's attitude about what happened to Bob changed. He realized his brother was right. In the face of overwhelming circumstances in that war, despite all the major screw ups, mishaps, confusion and mistakes, they had done the best they could. This was Bob's final gift to Lou. . . . . . . and to us. Now I understand why Lou had to tell me his brother's story.[6]

NOTES

1. The battles in and around Metz began in September and lasted for several weeks, ending in December. Lou believes Bob arrived late in the year, so it's likely he was wounded near the end of the battle. This would have been in late November or early December.

2. Since Bob was in and out of consciousness the time frames are necessarily approximate. It's likely this injury occurred in late February 1945, since there was heavy fighting near Bitburg then. The details about Bob's injury are from Bob's memory, shared much later with Lou.

3. The family learned the details of this from the seaman, who visited the family several years later.

4. Three of the original men in the platoon returned after recovering from injuries.

5. Bob never shared the details of what happened to him with his family. The night of Bob's funeral Lou sat down with Bob's wife and children and told them Bob's story.

6. The author interviewed Lou Boswell for this story on 4/7/10, followed up by a phone interview on 4/30/10.

■ ■ ■ ■ ■ ■ ■ ■ ■ ■

Chapter 16

Witness to Inhumanity

P aul Harris was born in Maryland and grew up there. He was studying Education in his third year at Towson University when he enlisted in 1942. He was allowed to finish his college term before being called into the Army. After several months of training he was assigned to the 65th Infantry Division. Much to his chagrin, this division was used as a cadre for replacements. Paul and many of the others wanted to get overseas, but they were being used to train others for overseas duty. Although his role was important to the war effort, he was frustrated, and his requests for overseas duty were turned down.

Paul was assigned to Service Company in the 261st Infantry Regiment. This company's role was to provide all the supplies to the regiment, including food, uniforms, equipment, and ammunition. His assignment was delivering munitions to the different companies. Originally a sergeant, he applied for, tested and was appointed to the position of assistant munitions officer. His rank was Warrant Officer Junior Grade (WOJG). Since he wasn't a commissioned officer he didn't have to attend Officer Candidate School, but still had many of the privileges of a commissioned officer and his pay was equivalent to that of a 2nd lieutenant.

Paul finally got his wish when his entire division left for overseas duty by troopship, in January 1945 and arrived in Le Havre,

Paul Harris at a destroyed German airfield
alongside a Messerschmitt 262 engine in 1945 (P. Harris)

France later that month. After additional training and an inspirational talk by General Patton himself, they were brought up to the front lines on March 9th, near Saarlautern, Germany. From then on, until the end of the European war in May, they were in combat. This division followed directly behind the fast-moving armored divisions. Paul and his men, in their 6x6 trucks, supplied ammunition to the companies in his regiment, sometimes traveling 50 miles or more between the ammo depots and the front line companies. It was often a 2-hour ride each way and they were constantly on the move.

On April 5th he came upon a sight he couldn't forget, a sight which would defy explanation even today.[1] The front lines were moving quickly. The Americans crossed the Rhine River a few days earlier and Paul and his men were in their truck, outside of the town of Ohrdruf, on another ammunition run. The 261st Infantry Regiment was close behind the 4th Armored Division. Paul smelled a terrible stench originating in an open field on their route. When he looked in the field he saw 30-40 dead men, dressed in tattered black and white striped clothing. A closer look revealed their hands were wired behind their backs. Each emaciated corpse had a bullet in the back of his head. Their positions clearly showed they had been forced to kneel before they were shot. It was a terrible sight and the men moved on, not understanding what they had seen, but realizing they had come upon the aftermath of a mass execution. What they had witnessed made them angry, the shooting of these poor, defenseless souls, whoever they may have been, were clearly non- combatants.

Close by they came upon a fenced camp. This was the Ohrdruf concentration camp, a sub-camp of Buchenwald. The German guards had already fled, taking most of the prisoners on forced marches. Many prisoners were executed outside the camp, such as those seen by Paul, and other dead and near-dead prisoners remained inside the camp. The armored unit had already called for assistance within the camp. He and his men passed by the fenced entrance and then continued on with their mission.

They had no idea camps like this existed. Paul later heard that some of the local civilians admitted they knew of the existence of the labor camp, but had no knowledge of what was occurring inside the fences. He also learned later that the Americans forced the local citizenry to visit the camp and witness what the SS had done. This was the first camp of its type in Germany liberated by American soldiers and both Generals Eisenhower and Patton visited the camp several days later. Many photos of the generals in the camp were later released to the Press, but by this time the 65th Infantry Division had left the area, following the armor unit.

Paul and his men continued on with their fast-paced duties, occasionally getting shelled, but always on the move, occasionally taking prisoners when they found them.[2] A month later they would witness a similar camp, but this time it would be up-close. They had crossed from Germany into Austria, again following another armor unit, the 11th Armored Division. During the first week of May they were stopped east of Linz, near the town of Enns. They heard of another camp just a few miles north of them, near the town of Mauthausen. This camp had been liberated by the armor unit a few days before and the Red Cross was already there, providing aid. Paul and two of his sergeants decided to take a jeep and drive over to see the camp. They heard the about the conditions at the camp, but nothing could have prepared them for what they were about to witness.

As they approached Mauthausen in their jeep, they were at the crest of a hill when they saw three men in striped clothing, little more than skeletons, at the base of the hill. The men were walking away from the reported location of the camp. Paul and his men drove down the hill and approached the three men, who were extremely weak and sickly-looking. They were speaking a language that Paul and his men didn't understand. They put them in the jeep and the men got very upset, trying to get out of the jeep. They clearly did not want to return to the camp, but Paul knew they needed to be there to get food and medical treatment. The Americans held them in the jeep, continued on their way to the camp and released the men to Red Cross workers inside the camp.

A terrible stench surrounded the camp as they approached. Red Cross workers were preparing soup and otherwise tending to the sick. There were piles of dead bodies inside the camp, stacked several high, just skin and bones, all wearing the same striped, tattered rags for clothing. Paul and the two sergeants walked into some of the sheds that had served as housing. Inside were skeletons lying on wooden planks that served for beds, some dead and others more dead than alive, unable to move. Those who were mobile were outside. The Americans walked into a building that served as the crematorium. It was still warm, with flesh inside. They were at the camp for less than an hour, but it made a permanent impression on the men.

The war in Europe had now ended, but Paul remained in Europe for another year. He left the Army on his return home, but stayed in the Army Reserves for three years. He married his 3rd grade sweetheart, Beatrice ("Bee"), six months after he returned home. While overseas a friend of his, Sven Magnusson, convinced him he should study accounting when he returned home.[3] He attended the Baltimore Institute, finishing as a CPA in 1949. He worked as a CPA in Baltimore for several years, first for an accounting firm and then for Kaiser Aluminum. He and his wife raised two sons and Paul was eventually transferred to California. He retired after 34 years

Paul Harris-recent photo (P. Harris)

with Kaiser and had his own accounting firm for three years as he transitioned into retirement. Beatrice died in 2002 and he recently remarried. Paul and his wife, Naomi, live in Concord, California.[4]

(Author's note: Many of our American ground forces in Europe saw evidence of the holocaust in various forms, bits and pieces of a larger even more horrific event. It was not until long after the war ended that the scope and magnitude of what occurred was known by these soldiers and by other Americans. From interviews with other veterans, I learned that many believed and hoped that what they saw, in all its horror, was a unique and isolated incident. Paul Harris had many interesting experiences in Europe, but he was kind enough to tell me about these two particular events. I chose to focus on them, since they are eyewitness accounts and we must not forget what happened.)

NOTES

1. It's possible this incident occurred late on April 4th. Harris recalled his unit was very close to the armored unit, at most a few hours behind them.

2. Although not included in this story, during this time Paul Harris was awarded the Bronze Star for bravery for crossing the Danube River, under fire, delivering ammunition to his troops.

3. Sadly, Magnusson was killed while crossing the Remagen Bridge in Germany.

4. The author interviewed Paul Harris for this story on 2/26/10 in Concord, California.

■ ■ ■ ■ ■ ■ ■ ■ ■ ■

Chapter 17

A Defining Moment

Ray Slominski was exhausted and hungry. He had been a prisoner now for nearly 2 ½ years. It was near the end for him in many ways. Since his capture in December 1942 he had been on a long, arduous journey. He spent two weeks in an SS hospital in Evreux, France and was then transferred to a hospital in Paris. From there he was taken to another hospital at Dulag Luft in Wetzlar, Germany for interrogation, then to the hospital at Stalag 9C in Bad Sulza, Germany. Next he was sent to Stalag Luft 3 at Sagan, then Stalag Luft 1 at Barth and then Stalag 7A at Moosburg. Finally, he was transferred to Stalag 17B near Krems, Austria, where he spent nearly 1½ years.

Ray Slominski at Stalag IXC in early 1943 (R. Slominski)

It was as if the Germans didn't know what to do with him. He was one of the first American airmen shot down over Europe. As the American Army Air Force became stronger, more planes and men were shot down, creating a need for more and larger prisons.

During his time at Stalag 17, Ray ran for office and won the election, becoming the Camp Librarian, with an inventory of 4,000 books, supplied by the Red Cross. He had a staff of 18 volunteer, part-time employees, all POWs, who helped him manage the book inventory. Having a job helped him pass the time. He had something else to think about and less time to focus on loneliness or contemplate his fate. His wounds slowly healed and he settled into POW life.

In early April 1945, prison staff made the decision to move the able-bodied prisoners out of the camp, as the Russians approached from the east. Their intent was to surrender to the Americans, who were advancing from the west. The men were divided into groups of 500. Most of the original guards had now been replaced by Volkssturm, older men who were conscripts, another sign of Nazi desperation. Twenty guards were assigned to his group and they began walking westward, on the north side of the Danube river, toward the American lines. Ray and the others knew the war was going well for the Allies. A clandestine crystal radio in their camp provided them with accurate news from the BBC. There were also visible signs in the air. Allied bombers and fighters roamed the skies freely now. If they could just hold out and avoid being mistakenly strafed by the American fighters, freedom could soon become a reality.

Initially the men were given Red Cross food parcels to take with them on the march. Ray teamed up with four of his buddies into a "combine", a mutual-support group to assist one another. Within a few days these supplies ran out. Ray was good at bartering, so he became the official barterer for his combine. The men pooled their pieces of soap, bits of chocolate and cigarettes left over from the Red Cross parcels and turned them over to Ray. He also had one distinct advantage over some of the other men. He spoke Polish. Many of the homes along the route had Polish housekeepers, young women taken from their homes and forced to work for the Austrians.

The men were not closely supervised so when the group entered a village or town there weren't enough guards to keep tabs on all of them and it was relatively easy to slip away. Ray would temporarily break away from the group and knock on a door, hoping to trade some of his meager stash for food. Often as not a young Polish housekeeper would answer the door, surprised that this young, dirty but friendly, bedraggled American could speak her language. Ray was usually successful in his efforts, particularly in trading his small pieces of soap or chocolate saved from the Red Cross parcels for bread or a piece of sausage. After the trade Ray rejoined the group, his absence undetected by the guards and the food would later be shared with his four friends.

Day after day the men continued walking, one step at a time, sleeping at night in barns or on the ground. Food was in short supply so the men were dependent upon Ray's bartering and the occasional bit of barley soup and bread supplied by their captors. Ray's combine fared better than some of the others, but the men were still cold and hungry.

After several days on the march Ray and his group approached the city of Linz and it was in this area that Ray made a decision that would have an impact on him and define him for the rest of his life. As the Americans walked down the road Ray saw a group of approximately 200 souls approaching them, walking in the opposite direction. The Americans were appalled by what they saw. This group was mostly men, but included several women and children, guarded by SS troopers. They were a group of skeletons, starving, with sunken, empty eyes, barely alive, with loose skin hanging on their bones. As the groups passed, Ray and his buddies tried to share their scraps of food, but those in the other group were too far gone and declined the offer. Some of the men in the group accepted cigarettes, but there was no interest in the proffered food.

One of the emaciated skeletons dropped to the ground in total exhaustion as he approached Ray. As soon as this happened, an SS trooper walked up, put his pistol to the back of the poor man's head and shot him. Ray's initial reaction was shock, quickly followed by intense rage, but he could do nothing. An overpowering thought entered his head that "the only good German is a dead German." He stopped himself right then. He knew he had to stop himself. He couldn't allow hatred to rule his life, even in his weakened state. Ray reflected on his years of imprisonment. Along with sporadic demeaning treatment there small were acts of kindness and those who helped him along the way. When he was shot down, German soldiers had quickly taken him to the hospital and saved his life. There was the German nurse who, when out of sight of prying eyes, tucked the sandwich beneath the covers at the hospital, patting him gently on the shoulder as she walked way. There was the wounded German soldier who, when lying on a stretcher alongside him on a railway platform in Paris, gave him a pack of cigarettes. As the corpse was loaded by other prisoners onto an oxcart, Ray forced himself to let go of this feeling of hatred for all Germans, but he would never forget what he witnessed on the road that day.

(Author's note: In a chance meeting with Bernat "Bernie" Rosner, co-author of An Uncommon Friendship *in early 2004, Ray learned this was a group from one of the subcamps of Mauthausen concentration camp. Bernie and Ray may have passed each other.)* [1]

A few days later Ray's group reached a forested area, where they set up camp and waited for the American troops to approach across the Inn River. Their food ran out several days before reaching the forest. Fortunately, some Red Cross parcels arrived after they reached the forest and the men were able to eat

Ray and Jean Slominski (R. Slominski)

again. Somehow the Red Cross found their location. One day they saw American tanks across the river. The next day American tankers crossed the river. Ray and his buddies were liberated by men from the 13th Armored Division. It was a joyful day for all of them.

The American tankers quickly rounded up the remaining German guards and told the freed POWs they could shoot any of the guards who had beaten the Americans or who had otherwise treated them brutally. Most of the guards were older men and the Americans, for the most part, in Ray's group hadn't been treated poorly by the guards. Ray was proud that none of the Americans in his group chose to exercise this option. The Americans had been on the march about 18 days when they were rescued during the first week of May 1945 and had marched nearly 200 miles. Within a few days the men were evacuated to France and then sent back to America.

Ray received a disability pension and was released from the military after his return home. He met his wife, Jean, soon after the war ended, and they were married. Ray chose to return to school and earned a degree from the University of North Dakota. He and Jean moved to California where Ray ran an insurance brokerage for many years in the San Francisco Bay Area and he and Jean raised their two daughters in Concord, California. After Ray's retirement he and Jean enjoyed various hobbies, including photography and traveling. Ray left us in 2006, but he will always be remembered for his smile and his kindness. He truly deserved his title "The Little Giant".[2]

NOTES

1. One of the marches is described in *An Uncommon Friendship*, a book co-authored by Bernat Rosner and Frederic Tubach. On 8/15/45 Ray provided a written statement to the Judge Advocate General's Department, War Crimes Office, in which he described treatment at the hands of his German captors at Stalag 17.

2. The source of this story is a series of interviews with Ray Slominski. The author interviewed him during the making of the documentary *lives beyond the war* on 3/13/04 and 3/14/04 and interviewed him again in Concord, California on 7/21/04. Additional specific information also came from Ray's personal, unpublished papers he wrote about his experience as a POW.

■ ■ ■ ■ ■ ■ ■ ■ ■ ■

Chapter 18

Low-level Mission to Holland

It was May 1, 1945 and the European war was coming to an end. John Gilcrest, a B-17 pilot in the 568th Bomb Squadron of the 390th Bomb Group, 8th Air Force, had already completed 28 combat missions. They flew from a base near Framlingham, England. His crew had been lucky thus far and the war was nearly over for John and his 9-man crew.[1] This mission for which they were being briefed wasn't like the others. It would be flown at near tree-top level.

Things hadn't started out well for John on his arrival overseas. He and his crew came overseas by troop ship and John brought with him eight bottles of good bourbon. It was not easy to get the good stuff, even at home, and he treasured it. He didn't put the bottles in his footlocker because he thought they might "disappear" enroute, so he brought them with him in his B-4 bag, a big, zippered bag that held his clothes and other essential personal items that remained close to him at all times. The bag was overloaded and heavy as he walked down the gangplank at Liverpool. Much to his horror the zipper gave way, spilling the contents. The bottles rolled down the plank and were quickly picked up and spirited away by some of the Brits on the pier. The

John Gilcrist and crew. John is in the back row, 2nd from left (J. Gilcrist)

war wasn't starting out well for John but, like many Americans he would improvise and would learn to drink scotch whiskey instead.

On what would have been his first mission all eight planes in his squadron were shot down by German fighters. The mission date was January 14, 1945. What saved him was their flight surgeon grounding the entire crew because four of the men had colds.

The crew had their share of close calls. You couldn't fly combat for very long without having your share and paying your dues. On February 26th they lost an engine over "Big B", Berlin, on one of the biggest 8th Air Force bombing raids of the war. More than 1200 bombers participated in the mission.[2] Fortunately, they had already dropped their bombs and the plane was lighter, allowing them to keep their speed and remain within the protection of the formation and make it home safely.

There was that mission to the Ruhr Valley on March 7th. They lost the #3 engine due to flak. They couldn't stop the engine from "wind-milling" causing a lot of drag and making the plane extremely difficult to fly. They couldn't keep up and were forced to leave the formation. The #3 engine caught fire, but they were able to extinguish it with the engine fire suppression system. There was intense vibration from the wind-milling engine, causing the right main landing gear to drop down, which created additional drag, and the fuel tanks were nearly empty when they reached the English coast. The engine caught fire again just prior to landing, but John was able to set the plane down safely.

On April 7th they bombed the Neumunster, Germany marshalling yards. On this particular mission John was leading his 3-plane element. Shortly after dropping their bombs John saw red and black flashes directly in front of his plane. Moments later he saw a Messerschmitt 262 jet fighter directly above him. It barely missed his plane and flew off without the gunners getting a shot at it. The tail gunner didn't even see the plane. The attack came from behind, out of the sun, from the 6 o'clock high position. Amazingly, they didn't receive a single hit as the proximity-fused 30 mm cannon shells exploded around them, but the plane in the #2 position on their right wing was hit. The fuel tanks on its left wing caught fire and it drifted out of formation and exploded. Once again they were lucky. John believed his plane, the element lead, was the likely target.

There had been a few other close calls, such as the time when John's seat was hit by a piece of flak that didn't penetrate a piece of armor plate, but mostly the crew had been very fortunate. Not one of them had been injured. By the third week of April it was announced there were no more strategic targets to be hit. The American and Russian ground forces were moving quickly and the targets remaining were smaller tactical targets, such as railways and bridges. These missions could best be accomplished by smaller numbers of medium bombers, flying at lower altitudes.

John flew just a couple such missions in late April. The B-17 was designed for high-altitude, strategic bombing. It was unusual for the men to be called upon for a low-level mission, but that would be their assignment on May 1st.

This would not be a bombing mission, but a mission of mercy to drop food supplies in Holland. When the Allied forces pushed their way into Germany, western Holland was cut off and by-passed. Thousands of German soldiers remained there. Amongst them, the Dutch people were starving. The dikes had been breeched and many of the fields were flooded. The Germans stopped sending supplies to the cities in Holland and the supply lines were cut. The situation was critical for the Dutch people. Many had already died of starvation.

The Dutch royal family approached the Allied powers and asked them to negotiate a truce with the occupying German military forces so food could be delivered to their starving countrymen. While the truce was still being negotiated, the British began dropping food supplies on April 29th, without being fired upon. A truce was agreed upon the next day.

On May 1st the Americans joined in. The Brits called it "Operation Manna". The 8th Air Force codenamed it "Operation Chowhound". They were dropping boxes of 10-in-1 rations, so named because there was enough food to feed 10 men for one day. John and his crew attended a briefing for the mission. All four squadrons of the 390th, each with 12 planes were participating in the mission. Several other bomb groups were also involved. The bomb bays in the planes were loaded with the food on a fabricated plywood platform that would be dropped in fields in pre-designated drop zones. Their designated zone at Valkenburg was marked with a large white cross so the crews could easily see it from the air.

The men were instructed to take no offensive action. This was a low-level mission, 500 feet or lower. They would come in over the drop zone low and slow. There were no parachutes on the food supplies and the boxes of food would be dropped directly onto the ground; hence the need to be as low as possible so the food supplies wouldn't be ruined or scattered over too large an area.

The planes took off, headed for Holland. They were flying directly into a German-held area. John wasn't concerned about this, but some of the men were likely apprehensive. After all, the Germans still had plenty of anti-aircraft guns. Even small arms fire could hit them at this low altitude. They needn't have worried.

As John's squadron took its turn, he saw men women and children on the rooftops of buildings and on the ground all around the drop zone. They were holding American and British flags, cheering and waving as he approached the drop site at tree-top level, dropping their precious cargo in the field. John's bombardier had no problem dropping the food on target from this altitude. What a great feeling!

German soldiers were also in view. They weren't cheering the Americans, but were also in need of food, cut off from their own supply lines. Some were running into the field to collect the food.[3]

The Dutch underground had saved many Americans and John had great admiration for them. Many risked their lives earlier in the war to hide downed American and British airmen and helped them to get safely out of Holland and back to England. On that day 396 8th Air Force bombers dropped 771 tons of food.[4] This was just the beginning of the operation.

John flew four more mercy missions to Holland. A total of six such missions were flown by his group. On May 5th and 6th he flew a mission to Ultrecht and on May 7th the drop zone was at Vogelenzang. While the first missions were flown in formation, on the later missions the planes came over the drop zone individually. On these missions the group flew in formation over the English Channel, but broke up and the planes flew single file over the former airfields and large, open fields designated as the "targets". Again the Dutch people were waiting for them, cheering and waving their flags. It made the men feel proud. It was a nice way for them to finish their war in Europe. John commented it was a thrill to be able to help the Dutch.

A few days later, after the war in Europe ended, the 390th Bomb Group was called upon for a different type of mercy mission. The American troops overran several concentration camps in Austria, filled with all different types of non-military prisoners from the occupied countries. The assignment of the 390th was to fly to a former German airfield just south of Linz, at Horsching, and bring planeloads of French and other European political prisoners back to France.

For this mission the gunners stayed home. Only the essential members of the crew necessary to fly and navigate the plane were aboard, in order for the maximum number of prisoners to be taken.[5] John was horrified to see the condition of the prisoners when he landed at Horsching. Many were French officials, who had been in nearby labor camps. He described them as "walking skeletons". Forty five of the freed prisoners were loaded into the plane. They were in the nose, on the flight deck, on a plywood platform in the bomb bay and in the rear of the plane. His #3 engine had a problem as he prepared for take-off so they had to take the former prisoners off the plane. There were no repair facilities at the field, so the flight engineer had to off-load several hundred gallons of fuel so the plane would be light enough to take off. They managed a 3-engine take-off and flew the plane back for repairs.

A couple of days later they returned to pick up more former prisoners. This time they completed their mission. Once again they crowded 45 men into the plane. One man even sat between the pilots. The overloaded plane managed to take off and they delivered the men to a field in France.[6] The former prisoners were full of lice. When they returned to base, both the crew and their

John Gilcrist-recent photo (Author's collection)

plane were sprayed with DDT to kill the lice that had spread to them and their aircraft.

John flew home to the U.S. in July 1945. He received his discharge from active duty several months later. John met his wife-to-be, Mary Ann, on a blind date shortly after he returned from overseas, while in southern California. They started dating and continued dating after John was discharged. John was born in Oakland, California but his family moved around a lot during his early years. He attended high school in Vallejo. After the war John enrolled at U.C. Berkeley and graduated with a Bachelor of Science degree in Engineering in 1950. He and Mary Ann married while he was still a student and they raised four children.

John worked for Kaiser Engineers for 36 years and at one point worked directly for Henry Kaiser. He stayed in the Air Force Reserve for 10 years after the war and was checked out in the P-51 Mustang, the same type plane that escorted him on many of the bombing missions. Mary Ann died in 2008. John lives in Lafayette, California.[7]

NOTES

1. At this stage of the war 8th Air Force crews had only 1 waist gunner, instead of the 2 that made up the 10-man crew earlier in the war. The single gunner manned both positions.

2. 8th Air Force Historical Society data indicates 1207 bombers and 726 fighters participated on the mission, in which three rail stations were bombed.

3. John heard later that some of the German soldiers were actually hit by the boxes of rations.

4. 8th Air Force Historical Society information.

5. The members of the crew on this flight were the pilot, copilot, navigator and flight engineer.

6. The aircraft wasn't as overloaded as one might think, since it's likely the former prisoners weighed less than 100 lbs. apiece. Still, the human cargo created crowded conditions.

7. The author interviewed John Gilcrest for this story in Lafayette, California on 4/6/10. Background information from John's memoirs, *My Military History: July 1942-September 1955* was also used.

Chapter 19

Tired, Just Plain Tired

Private Warren Jensen looked across the Elbe River that day in May 1945, near Barby, Germany and knew Russian troops were on the eastern side of the river. There hadn't been any firing for the past few days and it was relatively quiet. Warren was a gunner on a 10-man team that manned an 8-inch howitzer in the 793rd Field Artillery Battalion, part of the XIXth Corps. When it was announced over the radio that May 8th was going to be V-E Day and the European war was ending, it was not unexpected.

On that day the Soviet troops were celebrating wildly, shooting flares and mortars, and firing rifles on the other

Warren Jensen 1943 (W. Jensen)

side of the river. The sound of accordion music wafted across the river, intermingling with the other sounds. One would have expected it to be the same for Warren and his buddies, but there was no celebrating of any kind for this group of soldiers, no back slapping or shaking hands, no drinking, yelling or singing. They were simply too exhausted. Warren later described himself as being totally emotionally and physically depleted. They had no periods of rest since their landing 11 months earlier. They had been constantly on the move, without any breaks. In addition, the war was not over for them. Along with the news that V-E Day was at hand came the announcement that they would soon be redeployed to the Pacific to fight the Japanese. So they spent the day quietly.

Warren had come a long way since his enlistment in October 1942. A San Francisco native, he grew up and attended school there. His parents initially refused to sign the papers so he could enlist[1], but Warren was persistent and finally persuaded them to agree to his enlistment. He wanted to be in the field artillery and he got his wish. After additional training he went to Fort Bragg, North Carolina, where the 793rd Field Artillery was being formed and he became part of this unit. He became a gunner on an 8-inch howitzer crew. After additional training they deployed to England in January 1944 to await the invasion.

Warren awakened on June 6th to the roar of planes overhead. The sky was full of American war planes, all painted with white stripes, "invasion stripes", around their fuselages. Soon his unit was on the move to Southampton. Within a few days they were on an LCT (Landing Craft Tank) and headed for Omaha Beach, with a barrage balloon flying overhead. He was excited and anxious to get into the war. The crossing was rough. As they approached the coast of France they watched the *USS Texas* firing its big guns, supporting the infantry. There was smoke in the distance, clearly visible as they neared the beach. Warren's boat landed several hours after leaving England, near Vierville. The

793rd Field Artillery Battalion M-4 somewhere in France 1944
(793rd FA Battalion)

bow opened and his gun crew drove off the ramp into 4 feet of water in their M-4 tracked vehicle, towing their 8-inch howitzer. They made it onto the beach without any problems.

The M-4 used the same chassis as the famed Sherman tank, but didn't have the turret mounted on top. Instead it had an enclosed passenger compartment, where his gun crew traveled. Warren wanted to see what was happening, so he volunteered to man the 50-caliber machinegun mounted on top of the vehicle and he manned this position whenever they were on the move throughout the remainder of the war.

When they landed, there was still a lot of debris and destroyed vehicles. Hundreds of wounded Americans were lying on stretchers and as soon as the landing craft was emptied, the wounded were loaded aboard for transport back to England. There was still intermittent firing by the Germans with their heavy guns, but it was haphazard and nothing nearby was hit. His gun battery headed inland about 1 ½ miles, where they set up their howitzer in an orchard and began firing in the direction of

St. Lo. The target was a main road leading into the town. They had a range of 5-8 miles. They could fire at a rate of two rounds per minute.

On his first day in Normandy he saw his first German, a soldier killed during the invasion. It was just the first of many he would see in the next 11 months. Nearby fields were littered with dead farm animals. His unit was never far behind the infantry, at most a few miles and at times they were right on the front lines.

As the Americans advanced and the front lines moved, so did Warren and his unit. Sometimes they stayed in the same location for a few days, but often they moved daily, supporting the infantry's advance with their howitzers. They could never predict when they would be moving, at least not far in advance. Their gun was normally set up in an open field, with a clear field of fire, not in a village or city. As they progressed through France that summer and fall they slept in the open, digging foxholes for protection. They never had a complete night's sleep, even on those rare occasions when they weren't firing their howitzer. The team shared the responsibilities of guard duty and radio duty, so they slept in shifts, on the ground.

The summer turned to fall and they moved through France, Belgium and into Holland. The weather grew colder, but their living conditions remained the same. Warren recalls one fall night they spent in a house in Holland and it didn't seem right. That was the only night he slept inside until the war ended. They preferred to sleep outside now. They felt safer there. Fall turned to winter. There was the Battle of the Bulge with the horribly frigid weather, the inadequate clothing and the push into Germany.

Warren specifically remembered taking only three showers during this time, the first one just south of Paris. There was a military trailer set up with shower facilities for the American soldiers. The men formed a line outside. When they entered the trailer, they had about 30 seconds to shower, then a whistle blew and they went to a drying room in the trailer where they received new clothes, a wonderful luxury. His last shower was in Holland in early December 1944, just before the Battle of the Bulge. It would be the last time he bathed until after the war ended. It felt great if he could just change his underwear.

On and on they pushed, deeper into Germany, sleeping outside in the snow, sometimes in sub-zero conditions. They could generally have a fire in their foxholes during the day, but not at night for fear of attracting German gunfire. Sometimes they put wooden doors over the foxholes, covering them with dirt to shield them from enemy shrapnel. Most of the time they had decent food. The unit had a 2 ½ ton truck with a stove on it and the cooks used the stove to make the food and deliver it to the men. When they didn't get hot food there were usually plenty of K rations and C rations, so they didn't go hungry.

There were lots of memories of war. His unit pushed past some of the death camps that were recently liberated. The stench from the crematoriums was horrible for miles around these camps. Finally they reached the Elbe….and stopped. Warren was injured in April 1945 when a German ME 262 jet fighter strafed his position along the Elbe River, but it was a minor wound and he wasn't relieved of duty.

After V-E Day Warren decided to venture across the Elbe and hitched a ride in a jeep across a pontoon bridge constructed by the 2nd Armored Division. The Elbe was about 100 yards across at this point. No one from his gun crew accompanied him on this excursion. They were content to just relax. He was surprised to see the Soviet troops were a Mongolian infantry division and really tough-looking. They were shabbily-dressed and were obviously frontline troops. The artillery which accompanied them was horse drawn. The only Caucasians he saw were some large, strong Russian women soldiers directing traffic. These people didn't speak English and there wasn't a whole lot to see so he crossed the river again and returned to his buddies.

While awaiting transfer to the Pacific they were given other responsibilities. One of their tasks was locating Russian laborers who had been brought to this part of Germany when the Germans invaded Russia. The laborers were spread out on farms throughout the area. By agreement with the Russians, the laborers, both men and women, were brought to a central location. The laborers were then put in train boxcars and taken to a location in the Russian zone. Warren and others in his unit were assigned to accompany the Russians to a pre-arranged location in the Russian zone, a 2-day train ride. The American artillerymen were assigned a car and given rations to provide to the Russians. The train occasionally stopped and the food passed out. The laborers seemed to be in good spirits, happy to be going back to their homeland. The Americans weren't really guarding the Russians, who could have left the train had they wanted. The Americans were there to make sure they were safely turned over to the Russian troops.

Warren also guarded the Autobahn to insure that those traveling had passes. There was no vehicle traffic, but there were

Warren Jensen-recent photo (Author's collection)

hordes of people walking or pushing carts filled with their possessions. Since Warren didn't read German, nearly anything could suffice as a pass. They were particularly suspicious of young men. It was no secret that SS troops were trying to get out of the country to avoid prosecution, so young men were checked to see if there was a blood type tattooed on their arm, a sure sign they had been in the SS When found, they were turned over to the military police.

Even when V-J Day was announced there was no big celebration. Sure, the men were happy the war was over, but now they just wanted to return home and get on with their lives. Warren returned home in December 1945. He attended U.C. Berkeley on the G.I. Bill, graduating in 1949. While still a student he married his wife, Dorothy. He later obtained two Master's Degrees at San Francisco State. He worked for seven years as a manufacturer's rep for a steel company and then became a teacher and counselor at Woodside High School on the San Francisco Peninsula. Warren and his wife raised one daughter and they now live in retirement in Concord, California. After the war Warren received a commission in the Army Reserves, based on his combat experience and remained in an artillery unit, serving as a battery commander, retiring with a total of 23 years of service.[2]

NOTES

1. At that time one needed to be 21 years of age to enlist, unless a parent signed a statement agreeing to the enlistment.
2. The author interviewed Warren Jensen for this story in Walnut Creek, California on 1/31/10 and completed a follow-up phone interview with him on 2/8/10.

Chapter 20

The Best of America

As the Americans fought their way through faraway places in North Africa, Europe and a host of Pacific Islands they encountered people in their path, men, women and children who weren't combatants. Some were pro-American, some were anti-American and some were neither; many were just trying to survive.

Some of the men provided anecdotes of contacts with the civilians along the way. One of these is Vernon Jones. Vernon is a Philadelphia native, having grown up with three brothers and two sisters. His family was poor, but he never knew it, because other families around him were in the same situation. His parents both worked hard to put food on the table. His father was a

Vernon Jones after discharge
(V. Jones)

163

janitor and his mother a laundress. Working together, they managed to support their family during the Depression.

Vernon wanted to be a doctor. He managed to enroll at Wilberforce University in Ohio, studying pre-med.[1] He was also in ROTC. The plan was for him to become a doctor and then fulfill his obligation to serve five years in the Army. The war was in full force in 1943 and the Army had other plans for him.

At the end of his freshman year of college, he was inducted into the Army. The military was segregated then and the black troops were kept separated. After a couple of stops on the way he ended up at Fort Riley, Kansas, at the Cavalry Replacement Training Center. Here he took his Basic Training. His barracks sergeant was Joe Louis, the famous boxer. He still has memories of Joe, who was in excellent shape, taking the men on 5-miles around Rimrod, a man-made mountain, with many of the men falling out, unable to keep up with Joe or complete the run. (Vernon was athletic and managed to keep up.)

After additional training in Fort Clark, Texas he ended up in Troop A, 35th Cavalry Reconnaissance Squadron. His unit consisted of tanks, cavalry and armored cars. After additional training they were shipped overseas, first to Casablanca, then to Oran. They were unassigned and the Army didn't seem to know what to do with them. At Oran they became the 6483rd Car Company and it seemed their chief assignment was driving officers around. In Oran the unit became the 3821 Truck Company, 133rd Battalion and they were shipped by freighter to Naples, Italy to be truck drivers.

In Naples they went to pick up the trucks. Vernon was surprised to see the trucks assigned were semi-trucks. Vernon had never learned to drive before entering the service and certainly didn't know to drive a big truck. He quickly taught himself to drive the big behemoths, but had a difficult time backing them. This simply wouldn't do. Since Vernon had been working as supply sergeant, he knew what the captain's signature looked like.

He simply changed the orders, requisitioning 30 GMC 6x6 trucks, much easier to handle. No questions were asked. He and the others had no trouble driving these vehicles.

In Italy, the company had various duties. For a while they hauled gasoline for the 332nd Fighter Group at Ramitelli, the Tuskegee Airmen. They also hauled 155 mm ammunition up to the artillery units. Whatever needed hauling they hauled, sometimes in long convoys. When the war ended in Europe, there was still plenty of work for them.

They had moved up north to Livorno, another port on the west coast of Italy.[2] They received orders to retrieve German POWs who had been captured up in the Alps when the hostilities ended. They picked up the prisoners, 20 truckloads of them, and brought them back to a detention site. Vernon had a Thompson .45 caliber submachine gun in the truck with him, but there were no Americans on the trucks to guard the prisoners. MP's in jeeps were interspersed through the convoy in case there were any problems. They made five or six trips of this nature. On one of them an SS enlisted man asked to ride in the cab of the truck with him. The soldier spoke decent English, so Vernon allowed him to ride up front. There were no problems with the trooper. In fact, the men never encountered any problems with the German prisoners on these trips.

When their duties in Italy were finished, the company boarded the troop ship to take them home, or so they thought. They passed through the Mediterranean and into the Atlantic Ocean. Several days out to sea the water color changed from blue to green and Vernon could see seagulls, a sign that they were nearing land. The ship's captain announced they were docking in Panama and would be passing through the Panama Canal early the next morning. Now it was obvious they weren't returning home, but headed to the Pacific, to another war zone.

After a brief stop at Eniwetok Atoll in the Marshall Islands, they moved on to the Philippines. While in the Philippines they learned the war with Japan had ended. They still weren't going home, though. They boarded an LST (Landing Ship Tank) and sailed to Japan, now assigned to the 1st Armored Division. After temporary duty there, Vernon was finally able to return home. He arrived in the U.S. in December 1945 and was discharged shortly thereafter.

The war had interrupted his plans to become a doctor. On his return he decided to pursue a different career, that of a teacher. He enrolled at Lincoln University in Oxford, Pennsylvania. He graduated in June, 1949 with a bachelor's degree in Health and Physical Education.

In those days it was difficult for a black man to get a teaching job in Philadelphia. He was able to secure a teaching job in Maryland, where he worked in a black high school. He wanted to return to Philadelphia, so he moved back and took a couple of temporary jobs before getting a permanent job in the Philadelphia school system teaching 6th grade. Eventually he became an elementary school principal in Philadelphia. In 42 years as an educator he never took one day of sick leave. The children depended on him, just as his country depended on him and all of our other veterans during World War II.

Along the way, Vernon married. He raised three children, two daughters and one son. Eleven years ago after retiring from the school system, he moved to Walnut Creek, where he resides today.

During their wartime travels Vernon and his buddies had many opportunities to meet the civilian population. It started in North Africa and continued into Italy. In Naples, two orphaned Italian boys, ages 10 and 14, started hanging around the men. They were starving and had no means of supporting themselves. The men took them in, feeding, clothing and housing them. GI fatigues were altered to make clothes for the boys.

When they moved north, they took the boys with them and took care of them during the entire time the men were in Italy.

Vernon began teaching them English and the men learned Italian from the boys. The boys were also helpful to the Americans, translating for them and communicating with the locals when the trucks passed through towns, enroute to various destinations.[3]

There were other interactions with the civilian population in Italy. One day Vernon was invited to eat with a local family near Naples. They went fishing to catch their dinner. Vernon brought a couple grenades to assist with the fishing, casting the grenades into the Bay of Naples. Soon their boat was filled with fish, which were shared with the local fishermen, so all could have a good meal.

There were similar incidents in the Philippines and in Japan. In Japan, 30 young men were hired to work at the motor pool in Yokohama, which Vernon supervised. In addition, they hired two Japanese university students as translators and six young girls as maids and housekeepers. These were paid employees, earning wages and all were treated well. Vernon taught the girls to speak and read English and learned Japanese from them. All were fed while working at the base. GI clothes were sent to a nearby seamstress, who made the fatigues into clothes for the children.

The Allies set the policies and instituted overall plans at the end of the war, but it was the individual soldiers,

Vernon Jones-recent photo
(R. Slominski)

167

sailors, airmen and Marines who made the impressions on the local populations wherever they went. It was clear they came not as
conquerors, but as liberators and temporary occupiers. As
Vernon said "We Americans are not vindictive."[4] The kindness
and fairness of Vernon and other servicemen demonstrated the
best of America and its values and set the stage for the future.

NOTES

1. Wilberforce is the oldest, private black university in the U.S., founded in 1856, named in honor of William Wilberforce, an 18th Century abolitionist.

2. The Americans also know this city and port as Leghorn.

3. The boys wanted to return to the U.S. with the GI's, but this was not possible and Vernon lost touch with the boys when he left Italy.

4. The author interviewed Vernon Jones in Walnut Creek, California on 3/29/10, with a brief follow-up interview on 4/27/10.

Chapter 21

A Bird's Eye View of "Fat Man"

Frank Timmers wasn't happy with his squadron commander. It was August 8, 1945 and Frank was on Ie Shima Island, a P-51 fighter pilot in the 342nd Squadron of the 348th Fighter group. He sat in the office as his boss told him he was being taken out of combat. With 100 missions to his credit, his experience was needed to train new fighter pilots when as arrived from the States. He argued that he wanted to stay with his unit, but the commander wouldn't budge.

Frank arrived in New Guinea in January 1945. He was trained as a P-47 pilot, but the 348th was in the process of switching to the P-51 fighter when he arrived at Nadzab, New Guinea, so he transitioned to the Mustang and received his orientation for

Frank Timmers 1944
(Timmers family)

combat, flying a couple of missions to Rabaul. From New Guinea he went to the Philippines to join his unit which was engaged in the island-hopping campaign. His first combat mission was on January 20th.

The group had been in combat since the summer of 1943, starting out in New Guinea and had been very successful in battling the Japanese. There were several aces in the group. Many of the heaviest air battles took place in late 1944, just before Frank joined the group. When Frank joined his fighter group in the Philippines, the air battle for the Philippines was over and the group was heavily engaged in a ground-support role, dropping bombs and strafing Japanese forces in front of the American lines. Sometimes their bases were less than a 10-minute flight from the front lines, so close they had infantry perimeter guards to protect the airmen from infiltrators. During the month of April he flew 34 missions in 28 days.

There were still a few Japanese fighter planes in the Philippines, but Frank didn't see any. The P-51 was a great plane for dive-bombing and Frank became very adept in this role. The Japanese put up lots of 40-millimeter anti-aircraft fire, as well as smaller caliber fire, but Frank's plane was never hit by enemy fire. Others weren't so lucky and his squadron lost a total of 9 pilots during the time he was flying with them.

Typically smoke would mark their point of attack. The source of the smoke was often a smoke grenade dropped on the target by a single-engine observation plane, similar to a Piper Cub. After the smoke was visible to the pilots, the flight would begin their drive, generally from about 5000 feet. Frank used the nose of his airplane as the sight. He usually fired his 50-caliber machineguns to suppress any ground fire that was directly in front of him. At 2,000 feet he pulled out of his dive and dropped his bombs. The normal load was two 500-lb. bombs, one under each wing. It took some practice, but Frank and his buddies were good in their

Frank Timmers in front of P-51 1945 (Timmers family)

support role. Sometimes they would also strafe the targets after dropping their bombs.

After several months of combat in the Philippines, the group moved on to a base on the island of Ie Shima, off Okinawa and began flying missions in July.[1] No longer were they in the close support role, but were attacking ships in the South China Sea, as well as dive-bombing targets on the Japanese island of Kyushu, targets such as tunnels and anti-aircraft batteries. While on a dive-bombing mission to knock out two tunnels connecting Honshu to Kyushu he saw his first Japanese fighter plane. The date was July 31, 1945 and it was one of those maximum effort missions. There were more than 300 anti-aircraft batteries defending the tunnels. Unknown to Frank and the others in his squadron, the mission was called off due to bad weather while they were enroute to the target.

As they approached the target Frank entered his dive behind others in his flight, with his wingman trailing behind him. The wingman broke off his attack, due to the intense fire, while Frank continued on and dropped his bombs. Frank heard his wingman screaming for help, saying he was surrounded by Japanese planes. He spotted the wingmen several thousand feet above him, trying to outmaneuver 16 Japanese fighters. Frank climbed steeply, losing speed in the climb. He got one of the enemy fighters in his sights and began firing way out of range, to draw the attention on himself and away from his wingman. Only one of his guns fired and he rolled over, diving away from the fighters. His wingman was able to escape and the Japanese "Jack" fighters weren't able to catch either of them. That was his one and only encounter with a Japanese fighter. The mechanics checked the guns on his return to base and found someone had forgotten to load five of the guns.

Now, as Frank sat in his commander's office, he continued to beg and plead for someone else to be assigned to the training role. He wanted to be with the group to help support the invasion of Japan. The commander said he had already made the decision and Frank would be sent shortly to the Philippines to provide orientation training to these new pilots. The invasion of Japan was just a few weeks away and the new pilots must be ready for combat. As Frank sat there, realizing it was useless to argue his point, the phone rang and the commander answered it. The caller was the Lt. Colonel Bill Dunham, the deputy C.O. of the group. Dunham was the second leading P-47 ace in his group, with 15 or 16 kills and the fifth leading ace in the Pacific theater. Apparently four Japanese fighters had been shot down over Kyushu a couple days before and Dunham wanted to lead an unscheduled fighter sweep to try to find more Japanese fighters and was looking for a wingman. The squadron commander suggested he take Frank as his wingman, knowing how disappointed he was to be leaving the group.

On the morning of August 9, 1945 Frank took off with Lt. Colonel Dunham, headed for Kyushu Island. They were briefed on

Frank Timmers in P-51 cockpit 1945 (Timmers family)

the "no-fly" zones on Kyushu, areas which were apparently being attacked by other groups that day. They approached the island and were looking for Japanese fighters on the south side of the island, but weren't having any luck. About 11:00 am local time, Frank felt his plane shudder. He didn't know what was happening, but began banking. As he turned he could see the aluminum skin on his wings ripple and felt a series of concussion waves. When he looked down he also saw large rolling waves offshore, where before the sea had been relatively calm. As he looked off in the distance toward Nagasaki, he saw a huge cloud, shaped like a mushroom. He followed Dunham in the direction of the cloud, flying several miles until they were at the edge of the mushroom cloud and could see debris swirling in the cloud. They turned away and flew back to their base.[2]

On return they went to debriefing and told the intelligence officer what they had seen. They had heard of a big bomb dropped on Hiroshima a few days earlier and Frank suspected this was

Frank Timmers (R. Slominski)

another one of those big bombs. A few hours later his suspicions were confirmed when it was announced that an atomic bomb had been dropped on Nagasaki. The code name for the bomb, not known to the men at the time, was "Fat Man". That night Frank wrote home to his parents, not detailing what he'd seen, but telling them he thought the war was over and that the Japanese were crazy if they didn't surrender. Frank was right and the last mission for his group was on the 14th of September. There was no longer a need for him to instruct the new pilots.

The men were glad the war was over. He hated to think of the thousands and thousands of American lives that would have been lost if they had to invade. The dropping of those two atomic bombs saved a lot of American lives.

Frank returned to the U.S. in December 1945. A native of Berkeley, California he had grown up in nearby Albany. He remained in the Air Force Reserve for several years, continuing to fly the P-51 Mustang. He met his wife, Betty, who served in the Marine Corps, after he came home. He returned to U.C. Berkeley, finishing his degree in Forestry, and married Betty. He was in the lumber distribution business until he retired. He and Betty raised three daughters while living in their Lafayette, California home and were living there when Frank died in March 2005.[3]

NOTES

1. War correspondent Ernie Pyle was killed by Japanese machinegun fire on this island on 4/18/45.
2. Frank believed the no-fly zone was a 45-mile radius around Nagasaki and estimated he was nearly 100 miles away when he saw the cloud, before flying several miles toward Nagasaki.
3. Frank was interviewed for this story in Concord, California in July 2004

■ ■ ■ ■ ■ ■ ■ ■ ■ ■

Chapter 22

And Then They Occupied...

As soon as the war was over U.S. troops began to return home. Some returned more quickly than others, based on a variety of criteria, as well as the luck of the draw. For many a point system was used to determine how quickly they returned home, based upon such things as length of service, time overseas, and decorations. While most were returning home, yet others were being shipped overseas. One of those shipped to Europe was Lou Satz.

Lou, a Chicago native, was drafted into the Army in the summer of 1945. In late 1945 he was shipped to Europe to be part of the Army of Occupation. His first assignment was with the 5th Infantry Regiment in Ebelsburg, Austria, which later merged with the 4th Constabulary Regiment. These men were responsible for law and order in their region.

Lou Satz in Austria 1946 (L. Satz)

Austria had been divided into different zones, with the individual Allied country's military forces policing their respective zones. One of Lou's responsibilities was guarding the boundary between the Russian and American zone. He had a variety of other duties, which included watching for suspicious activity, whatever that might be. He also investigated criminal matters and black market activities and at one point escorted a trainload of displaced persons and former German soldiers.

There were an estimated 400,000 displaced persons in Austria when World War II ended. These were people forcibly removed from their various countries overrun by Germany during the war and then forced into labor in Austria. Many had been in concentration camps. Thousands of these people were still in the camps when Lou arrived, as the Allies tried to determine how to deal with the situation. Most were diseased and in poor health. Many no longer had homes to which they could return or did not want to go back to their homelands, especially those whose countries were now under Russian control.

Lou had many fascinating experiences during his year in this war-ravaged part of Europe. One he described in his book, *Occupation Europe: 1945-1946, As Witnessed by a 19 Year-Old GI*. The following story is just one of them, told in Lou's own words from his book.

****

One late afternoon in early October, I was in the orderly room when First Sergeant Bob Noble came in and asked me what I was doing there on Yom Kippur eve instead of attending services. I explained that I was on duty and that there wasn't a synagogue within 60 kilometers. Sergeant Noble suggested that I get into his jeep and go up the road five kilometers to the Jewish displaced persons camp where he was certain they were conducting services. With that, Sgt. Noble tossed me the keys to his jeep and off I went. What a thoughtful man!

I drove to the DP camp. It had barbed wire fences, guard towers and heavy, unpleasant odors, dirt floors, and no privacy for inmates. I walked towards a gathering of men only, led by an ancient rabbi in full orthodox regalia. Suddenly a young woman speaking fluent English wanted to know how I dared interrupt the services for which they had permission. In fact, I had interrupted the services. The rabbi suggested I lead them in prayers, but upon learning that I didn't know how, he insisted that I stand at his right elbow, a place of honor. I stood at his side and when the service was over, every single person in the camp, over 200 people, wished me a Happy New Year and hugged me. What an emotional feast! I was overwhelmed.

As long as I remained in Austria, when my workday was over, I went to the same DP camp. I brought food, clothing and medical supplies. I wrote many letters on behalf of the survivors to their relatives in the U.S. and I worked with a United Nations agency (UNRRA), whose mission was to relocate DP's and attempt to reunite families. Soon, some of my buddies were bringing in sheeting and plumbing supplies to help make the survivors' lives more comfortable. It was a very meaningful experience and resulted in my lifetime personal interest in the Holocaust and its victims.

Many years later, when I was a publishing executive, the president of my company called me into his office and said, "Lou, next month one of the great heroes of the 20ᵗʰ Century will be coming to New York City."

He was talking about Simon Wiesenthal, hunter of Nazi war criminals that had committed horrible crimes against civilization. He had written the book The Murderers Among Us. *This was Simon Wiesenthal's memoir which would be published by McGraw-Hill, first in hardcover and later in paperback by my company, Bantam Books.*

My assignment was to arrange a cocktail party for Wiesenthal and the senior people of the two companies. When Wiesenthal entered the room, he struck an imposing figure. You could feel the strength of this man. I was standing with about six people in a half circle when Wiesenthal was brought to the group by the editorial chief. Each of them

Lou Satz with Ray Slominski, the "Little Giant" (L. Satz photo)

shook hands and exchanged pleasantries. But soon the two of us had a chance to talk.

You know, Mr. Wiesenthal, I've been to your country," I said.

"When? Where?" he asked.

I told him the story of Bob Noble and my experience on Yom Kippur. He looked at me quizzically and suddenly embraced me. There were tears streaming down his cheeks. "You were the young soldier who came to us that night? he asked. "Do you know how you raised our spirits and gave us inspiration?"

The two of us embraced with strength and tenderness, and cried in the middle of a room filled with people. The event was one of the most meaningful, emotional nights in my life. I have related this incident many times and often people react with great emotion and often tears. [1]

****

So, many Americans remained in Europe and Japan. Plans were in place to rebuild these countries. Our government formulated the plans in conjunction with our allies, but it was the soldiers who set them in place and made them work. Along the way the Americans took time to make friends and influence the world in many other ways.

Lou returned home in 1947, where he finished his studies at the University of Illinois. He pursued a career in the book industry, eventually becoming the Vice President of Sales and Marketing for Bantam Books, a position he held for 25 years. Lou also acted as a consultant for other publishing houses. He raised two sons. Lou moved to California after retiring and lives in Walnut Creek.[2]

NOTES

1. This story is reprinted, with permission, in its entirety from Lou Satz's book *Occupation Europe; 1945-1946, As Witnessed by a 19 Year-Old GI*.

2. The author interviewed Lou Satz for this story during the filming of *lives beyond the war* on 3/13/04 and 3/14/04, with a supplemental phone interview on 4/27/10.

Epilogue

The lives of these men you've read about didn't end when World War II ended. It was a brief, but profound period in their lives. They went on with their lives and continued to build the world around them, most raising families, all contributing to their communities in various ways. Collectively they saved the free world. Individually they were men with principles who believed so intensely in freedom that they were willing to risk their lives.

Recently many of these men came to the aid of one of the members of their group. One of the younger men in the group was diagnosed with a late stage (stage 4) of throat and neck cancer. Just as they have answered the call many times in the past, they came to the aid of their friend in need. I am that friend.

It was pretty upsetting that day when I got the bad news from my doctor. I was working on several of the stories for this book. I had just finished a draft of a story about Bill Armstrong and gave it to him a day or two earlier to critique. Bill phoned late in the afternoon to provide feedback. During our conversation I didn't tell him of the diagnosis. As we talked about the story he sensed something was wrong. He asked if I was preoccupied and I reluctantly told him of the doctor's findings. Bill said he'd be over in an hour or so. I told him Ann and I planned to spend the evening quietly. To the best of my recollection, Bill's response was "Nonsense! You're not going to be alone tonight."

Bill came over that evening and gave his precious time. Bill's wife, Vera, wasn't doing well, but he still took time to spend time with Ann and me. Bill's son-in-law was also battling throat cancer and Bill reassured me my battle could be won. He was light-hearted, but serious and said he would be there for us………..and he was.[1]

Within days I started receiving cards and phone calls from the men. The cards had meaningful personal notes. The calls were uplifting, caring and had a calming effect on me. Several of them were living with cancer and other life-threatening issues, but they still took the time. I've grown to understand how precious time is.

I have lots of great friends and family who have all been supportive. I was never alone, but this group really inspired me. One of the issues that bothered me throughout my struggle was my promise to Ray Slominski, before he died, to write the book about him and this wonderful group, the Third Thursday Lunch Bunch.

There was no possibility of working on the book after my diagnosis. I had surgeries to insert a feeding tube and a chemotherapy port, for starters. This was followed by a combination of chemotherapy and daily radiation treatments. Much to my chagrin, I became too sick to attend the monthly meetings.

The calls and cards continued. Bob Tharratt phoned shortly after my diagnosis to tell me he understood it was a rough time for me, but he and his wife, Jeane, were praying for me and to just ask if I needed anything. I told Bob how sorry I was that I couldn't continue working on the book. Bob said Ray would understand and said there would be time later to finish the book. I wasn't so certain.

Lou Satz phoned me regularly. During one of our conversations he told me I had inspired him. I inspired him?!! I was sick as a dog, getting weaker by the day. I wasn't about to quit, but I certainly didn't think of myself as being able to inspire anyone.

One day a message was left on our message machine while I was at the hospital getting a dose of chemo. The message was Tom Morgan. Tom said he just finished reading one of my books for the second time and wanted me to know how much he enjoyed it. I couldn't have received a nicer compliment and it came when I needed a boost. His message also reminded me of the unfulfilled promise.

Ann had to take some of the calls for me. I was losing my voice as the radiation treatments continued and it was becoming extremely painful to talk or even swallow. Ann was always so nice to the guys, telling them I couldn't come to the phone and offering to take a message. Couldn't come to the phone? Hell, I couldn't even sit up in bed, but she was technically right, I couldn't come to the phone. The messages from the men were appreciated, but each was a reminder of that promise.

One important call came in December. I continued to receive monthly reminder calls about the luncheon meetings, as do all the members of the group. There is a list of all members and the list is divided up among certain members, who are the designated callers, to remind everyone of the meetings. John Tom had the list at the end of the alphabet with my name on it. Ann received the call and took a message. She came into the bedroom and said John phoned to remind me of the meeting. She politely told him she didn't think I'd make it to the meeting. MAKE IT TO THE MEETING?! Here I was, coughing up blood, unable to talk, swallow, eat or think clearly, with a feeding tube sticking out of my stomach. I was lucky if I could even make it to my own funeral!

During a calmer moment I realized John and the others knew I couldn't attend the meeting. It was just their way of letting me know they were thinking of me and that I was still important to them. Thanks, John.

As time progressed I regained enough strength for the next surgery, the main one, on my neck. I was scared. Bob Tharratt again came to my rescue. He invited Ann and me to attend church with him and Jeane. I hadn't been going out and my clothes didn't fit, after extensive weight loss (40+ lbs at that time) but we attended church with them. It had a calming effect on me. A priest from Bob's church, St. Paul's Episcopal, came to the house to meet with us the day before surgery. Ann and I are both grateful for this support.

There were other ups and downs along the way. I developed an infection after the surgery and my condition weakened. Months later I was still getting my reminder calls from John Tom. I was pretty weak, having lost more than 60 lbs. now and wasn't getting out much. The unfilled promise was constantly on my mind, accompanied by a certain amount of guilt. I looked different after the weight loss and the scarring from the surgery. I wanted to see my friends. I promised John I'd try to make it to the meeting.

I got up the day of the meeting, but didn't feel well. I wanted to go to the meeting, but told Ann it wasn't a good day and I just didn't know if I could make it. Ann planned to give me a ride to the Denny's Restaurant in Concord for the meeting. I was still too weak to drive. When it was time to leave, I told Ann I wasn't feeling well and suggested we'd better wait a little while. An hour later I felt a little better so Ann dropped me off at the restaurant.

I was self-conscious when I walked into the banquet room. The men, 40 or more of them that day, were busy eating and visiting when I walked in. I feared that most of them wouldn't recognize me, but Bob had seen me recently and he would know me. I needn't have worried. Bob saw me, got up and approached me. Some of the others also noticed the newcomer. There were signs of recognition from a couple of my friends. A few men started clapping and soon the whole group was clapping. Several of the men got up from their tables and came over to shake hands or hug me. I was totally overwhelmed. Bob asked me to say a few words to the group. I have no recollection of what I said, but I cried later that day.......and vowed again to keep my promise.

These men continue to inspire me. I've borrowed some time in my journey to finish this book. Thank God these men were there when our country needed them.................and when I need them. This fulfills my promise to my friend Ray Slominski, "The Little Giant", and it is also my gift to this special group of American veterans. I hope you've enjoyed their stories.

—Jerry Whiting

NOTES

1. Bill's son-in-law lost this struggle with cancer a few months later. Bill recently apologized for dodging the issue when, at one point, I inquired about his condition. Bill felt the news might depress me and I didn't need that. In retrospect, I think he was right.

Appendix A

Poem by Frank Tiscareno (1934-2001)
for
Technical Sergeant Bob Tharratt
United States Army Air Force
(Presented on November 11, 2000)

The savage battles high in the sky,

Lost in the past, so long, long ago,

When cannons tore metal, and frightened souls,

In box formations, both high and low.

And the Midland fields, where bombers sat,

Near concrete runways, in a constant roar,

With lines of breakfast at half past three,

And gunners cleaning the guns of war.

Green flares filled the air, and wheels rolled,

As heavy Fortresses began their climb,

And created formations in darkened skies,

As some thought of the calm they left behind.

Through clouds of flak and Messerschmitts,

When engines were lost, and bodies torn,

And all that was left was to get out,

And fall through a sky, the clouds adorn.

But safety was brief, and landings hard,

And a Stalag life waited up ahead,

Where cells were cold, and cells were dark,

And only wooden boards made up a bed.

And those who lived, and came back home

Still hold the memories of the deadly flak,

Remembering the battles, back in the past,

And thinking of those who didn't get back.

Appendix B

(*Author's note: Bill Armstrong was an ammo truck driver in the 26th Infantry Division and a story about him is in Chapter 11. Bill assembled a series of letters he wrote to his wartime buddy, Don Newlin, into a book called* Dear Don: Letters to a Wartime Buddy. *I love his writing style and thoroughly enjoy his stories. He has allowed me to include one of his "letters". In this letter he describes the crossing of the Rhine River in early 1945.*)

Dear Don,

What did you find to hide under the night we were waiting to cross the Rhine River? I ask because so much ordnance was being fired nearly straight up at the German aircraft that it was raining back down on us. After some shell fragments hit our ammo truck and a few small pieces had bounced off our steel helmets, Bob and I crawled under the truck. You and the captain were in an open jeep, so what did you find to hide under? There's not much room under a jeep.

I thought it was the greatest pyrotechnic show I'd ever seen. To peek out from under the truck was irresistible, a dumb thing to do, but a show like that comes once in a lifetime. With all that fragmentation and small arms pelting us, catching a piece in the forehead could have guaranteed that it was once in my lifetime.

It was fortunate that the German bombers missed the bridge and were driven off by our anti-aircraft fire. Once the firing had stopped the night became quite dark, which was fine with me. Just so it remained that way while Bob and I crossed the bridge. Ack-ack must have illuminated the scene for the fliers and the next time their aim might improve.

Bill Armstrong in Germany

Crossing was a slow process. Long lines of vehicles of every description waited to approach the pontoon bridge. Sorting out the priority must have been a real chore. Once our cannons had crossed, the ammo trucks had to be next or the batteries couldn't shoot. All the ammunition trucks had full loads; some of us were carrying over-loads. Once across the Rhine what we carried had to sustain the batteries. Until traffic crossing the pontoon bridge thinned out, we could not get back to the supply depots for more.

Word was passed down the line that we could cross soon and to get the engines warmed. We inched forward until we came to the ramp leading down to and onto the bridge. I have to admit that I was nervous about going out onto the two channels for the tires, but a soldier was there to guide us. The trucks were metered onto the bridge so there was a space of about thirty feet between the vehicles. The knowledge that I couldn't swim contributed to my anxiety, but once on the bridge I saw a sight that calmed me down. The engineers who had built the bridge took no chances and had stationed men with rifles in the inflated pontoons. They faced upstream to shoot any floating mines that the Germans might have dropped in the river. As we passed slowly by each pontoon I saw that one of the riflemen slept while his partner watched for the mines. I thought that if these guys can sleep out here I can forget my fears and enjoy the ride.

A few nights before the crossing, Bob and I had gone for a load of 105's and while returning to the batteries, came across something unusual. We were creeping along at the blackout speed of five or six miles an hour when a large shape loomed out of the darkness. It was so huge that whatever it was took up most of the road. We got out to determine what the thing was. It wasn't until we were a few feet from it that we saw a propeller. Bob thought it was a small landing craft to take the troops across the Rhine. It was on a tractor-trailer rig that was abandoned. There was nobody in the cab. While walking back to our truck, a very soft voice, almost a whisper, asked from above us, "Are you guys Americans?"

I looked up and saw a small white object floating above us. "Yeah, we are." Our nearly invisible interrogator sighed with relief. "Please wait. Don't leave. I'll be right down."

When he joined us I saw that he was a sailor. The white object was, of all things to wear in a combat zone, his sailors hat!

He told us the truck had broken down and he had been left alone as guard while the others went for help. He had no idea where he was and he was scared to death. I told him he'd better put on a steel helmet and get rid of the white hat before a German sniper used it for a target. This kid hadn't been told where he was going or that it could be dangerous. He had just come from the States and had no combat experience.

He hated to see us leave and asked if we could stay until the others returned. That wasn't possible, so after giving him a pack of cigarettes and telling him not to light up unless there was someplace on his boat under cover, we wished him good luck and went on our own way.

Someone was sure messing up, sending those green kids into combat conditions without preparing them for what was to come. I hope he lived to tell his story to his grandkids.

Bibliography

Armstrong, William C., *Dear Don: Letters to a Wartime Buddy*, Walnut Creek, California: Private printing, 1998

Armstrong, Vera, with Bill Armstrong, *BEPA, (Vera): An Autobiography*, Walnut Creek, California: Private printing, 1998

Blakely, Major General H.W.,*The 32nd Infantry Division in WWII*, Nashville, Tennessee: The Battery Press, Inc., 1957

Bussell, Norman, *Liberated Body, Captive Mind: A World War II POW's Journey*, New York, New York; Pegasus Books, 2008

Gilcrest, John, *My Military History: July 1942-September 1955*, Lafayette, California: Private printing, 2008

Public Relations Division-32nd Infantry Division, *13,000 Hours: Combat History of the 32nd Infantry Division-WWII*, 2773rd Engineers Printing

Rosner, Bernat and Turbach, Frederic C., *An Uncommon Friendship*, Berkeley, California: University of California Press, 2001

Satz, Lou, *Occupation Europe 1945-1946: As Witnessed by a 19-Year Old GI*. Walnut Creek, California: Louis K. Satz and Associates, 2007

Tharratt, Robert, *I Want You for the U.S. Army* (a personal memoir). Walnut Creek, California: Private printing.

322nd Bomb Group Association, *The Annihilators, 322nd Bomb Group (M): Book II, A Memoir Continued.*, Carrollton, Texas: IMPACT Advertising & Marketing, Inc.

Zaloga, Steven J., *U.S. Tank and Tank Destroyer Battalions in the ETO) 1944-45 (Battle Orders)*. Oxford, England: Osprey Publishing, 2005.

Lunch Bunch Attendance Roster

(With Unit affiliation, if known)

Armstrong	Bill	26th Infantry Division WWII
Bailey	Dick	322nd Bomb Group WWII
Beddia	Paul	U.S. Army-Armor
Behring	David	Honorary member
Boomer	Phil	Merchant marine WWII
Boswell	Louis	104th Infantry Division WWII
Brooks	Keith	86th Infantry Division WWII
Brown	Lewis	Navy Atlantic fleet Korean War
Cambridge	Jeff Arnet	565th Engineer Battalion Korea
Catalano	Tom	37th Infantry Division WWII
Chan	Ben	32nd Infantry Division WWII
Chenevey	Jim	99th Infantry Division WWII
Christensen	Bruce	Honorary member
Cram	Steve	U.S. Army Medivac pilot Vietnam
Denison	George	U.S. Army-Pacific WWII
Denny	Herman W.	U.S. Navy-YMS WWII
Dunn	Dan	Honorary member
Engstrom	Warren	32nd Infantry Division WWII
Ennis	Bill	Vietnam vet
Enrio	John	Unknown service
Everette	Oliver	U.S. Navy
Ezersky	John	747th Tank Battalion WWII
Fant	Glenn	U.S. Navy pilot-Vietnam
Farry	Bill	U. S. Army, ETO, WWII
Foltz	Ralph	U.S. Navy pilot-WWII

Fries	George J.	32nd Infantry Division WWII
Ganitch	Mickey	U.S. Navy WWII
Gilcrest	John	390th Bomb Group WWII
Graham	Chet	82nd Airborne Division WWII
Griffin	Griff	4th AAA Battalion, RAF
Groeper	Al	81st Infantry Division WWII
Guevara	Joe	98th AAA Battalion WWII
Gusey	Dick	U.S. Navy-legal yeoman
Harris	Paul R.	65th Infantry Division WWII
Hendrickson	Verle G.	U.S. Navy submarines
Hill	Stan	Tech rep-7th Air Force WWII
Hoskins	Harold K.	Tuskegee Airman-170th FG
Howard	Robert (Bob)	U.S. Navy Submarine Service
Hunter	Rip	Honorary member
Hunter	Rich	Honorary member
Ingraham	Dick	104th Infantry Division WWII
Jaworski	Dan	25th Infantry Division Vietnam
Jensen	Warren	793rd Field Artillery WWII
Jones	Vernon	3821 Quartermaster Truck Co. WWII
Kite	Alan	U.S. Navy Tactical Air Control Korea
Komor	Leonard	1326th Combat Cargo, 14th AF WWII
Looker	Neil	Honorary member
McKay	Robert (Bob)	58th Bomb Wing WWII
Massaro	Fred	58th Bomb Group WWII
Melikian	Clifford	42nd Infantry Division WWII
Mohan	Rod	U.S. Infantry Korea
Morgan	Tom	200th Infantry Division WWII
Mortenson	Earl W.	955th Field Artillery Battalion WWII

Murray	Jim	U.S. Navy DD885 Korea
Myers	Dean	USN Aviation Supply ship WWII
Nau	Henry	Air Force Intelligence WWII
Opelski	Frank	Civil Air Patrol
Parker	R.J.	533 MIS Battalion
Parrish	Fonzie	USS Pine Island WWII
Posey	Larry	13th Airborne Division WWII
Robinson	Harry	Civilian POW-Philippines WWII
Rogers	Dale	USS Sailfish WWII
Santacroce	Marc	USAF Vietnam
Satz	Lou	4th Constabulary Regiment WWII
Simmons	Duane	USAF post-WWII
Snider	Richard	12th F.A. Battalion
Spector	Arthur	USAF MATS 2001st AACS
Spencer	Ernest R.	100th Bomb Group, 8th AF WWII
Sperling	Richard (Dick)	1st Aviation Brigade-Vietnam
Tharratt	Bob	96th Bomb Group, 8th AF WWII
Thompson	Donald C.	Civilian POW-Philippines WWII
Townsend	John	US Navy pilot 1950-1963
Tom	John	71st Infantry Division, 66th Reg WWII
Tulk	Robert	U.S. Navy troopships WWII, Korea
Turkington	Martin E.	75th Infantry Division, WWII
Walker	Randy	USAF 87th Air Base Squadron
Whiting	Jerry	Honorary member
Williams	Robert	U.S.N. Deck Officer, WWII
Williams	Stuart	446th Bomb Group, 8th AF, WWII
Wiscavage	Chuck	USAF-Korea
Wood	Dave	California National Guard

INDEX

A

Aachen, Germany, 99, 130

Admiralty Islands, 52

Afrika Korps, 41, 57

Albany, CA, 174

Allen, Ernest , 89, 91-94

Allen , (General), 130, 131

Aloha Tower , 12

Alsace, 117

American Red Cross, 23

Amtrac, 72 , 77

Angaur Island, 75-77 ,80

Antioch, CA, 25, 26

Ardennes Forest, 98, 99, 105, 106

Ardoch, ND, 35

Armstrong , Bill , 89-96, 112 , 183, 191

Armstrong , Vera, 95, 96, 191

Arracourt, France, 91

Atape, New Guinea, 54

Atwater Kent radio, 26,

Australia, 43, 44, 50, 52, 56, 80

Austria, 32, 90, 95, 96, 137, 141, 143, 152, 177-179

B

Baccarat, France, 117

Bad Sulza, 141

Bailey, Dick, 97-104

Baltimore, Institute, 139

Bangkok, Thailand, 62

Bangor, ME, 61

Bank of America, 25

Bantam Books, 179, 181

Barby, Germany, 155

Barth, Germany, 141

Bassingbourne, England, 35

Bastard Battalion, 67, 69

Bay of Naples, 167

Beauvais, France, 97

Belgium, 71, 72, 97, 99, 106, 107, 112, 125, 158

Benson, MN, 59

Berkeley, CA, 14, 23, 29, 51, 54, 57, 90, 121, 153, 161, 174, 175, 191

Berlin, Germany, 148

BIA – Bureau of Indian Affairs, 65

Binghamton, New York, 103

Bitburg, Germany, 127, 133

Bitche, France, 117-119

Boswell, Bob, 126-133

Boswell, Lou, 125-133

Boswell, Richard, 126-128

Brehl, Ralph, 2, 3, 7

Brenner, Sy, 120-121, 123

Brisbane, Australia, 50, 52

Kaiser, Henry, 153

Kahului, 9, 14

Kalamazoo, MI, 47

Kansas City, KS, 105

Klamath Indian Reservation, 26

Krems, Austria, 141

Kwanghan, China, 62-64

Kyushu Island, Japan, 57, 63,
171-173

L

La Cambe, France, 69

Lakota Sioux, 32,

Lawrence, KS, 27

LCT – Landing Craft Tank, 67,
156

Leghorn, Italy, 168

Le Havre, France, 106, 135

Leyte Gulf, 22, 57

Liege, Belgium, 106

LIFE Magazine, 45,6, 48,

Lincoln University, 166,

Linz, Austria, 137, 143, 152

Liverpool, England, 147

Livorno, Italy, 165

Louis, Joe, 164

LSI - Landing Ship Infantry, 54

LST-Landing Ship Tank, 56, 76,
77, 166

Ludwigsburg, Germany, 120

Luzon, 17, 22, 55-57

M

Maastricht, Holland, 71

MacArthur, Douglas, 19, 45

Maginot Line, 117

Magnusson, Sven, 139, 140

Manila, 17-20, 22

Marrakech, 61

Marseilles, France, 115

Marshall Islands, 165

Martinez, CA, 2, 23, 112, 113

Maui, Hawaii, 9, 13

Maui Conference of Churches 9,

Maunalua Ridge, 10

Mauthausen camp, 138, 144

McKay, Bob, 59-66

McKay, Helen, 65

Melger, Arno, 91

Memphis Belle, 36, 41

Mendel, Charles, 37, 41

Metz, France, 126, 133

Minnesota, 59, 65, 115

Minnesota, Benson, 59

Missouri, 26

Modesto, CA, 90

Montclair, CA, 51

Moosburg, Germany, 141

Moraga, CA, 58

Morgan, Tom, 115-123

Muhlberg, Germany, 123

Munich, Germany, 85

Muscular Dystrophy Assoc., 48

N

Nadzab, New Guinea, 169

Nagasaki, Japan, 65, 173-175

Naples, Italy, 164, 166, 167

Navajo, 27

Navajo Indian Reservation, 27

Naval Weapons Station,
  Concord, CA, 96

Neuf Maisons, France, 117

Neumunster, Germany, 149

New Caledonia, 81

New Guinea, 29, 43-47, 50-52,
  54, 56, 169, 170

New York City, NY, 48, 72, 179

New Zealand, 80

Nichols Field, 17-19

Nisei, 120

Noble, Bob, 178, 180

Normandy, 67, 158

North Dakota State College, 59

Northwestern University, 14

Nuremberg, Germany, 2, 85

O

Oahu, Hawaii, 9

Oakland, CA, 51, 121, 153

Officer Candidate School, 75,
  135

Ohrdruf, Germany, 136, 137

Okinawa, Japan, 26, 29, 30, 171

Oklahoma, 26, 27

Omaha Beach, 67, 69, 156

Operation Chowhound, 150

Operation Manna, 150

Operation Nordwind, 115, 122

Oran, Algeria, 164

Oregon, 26, 27, 105

Orschiedt, Helmuth, 41

Oxford, PA, 166

P

Palau, 75

Panama Canal, 165

Paris, France, 121, 141, 144, 158

Parrish, Fonzie, 26, 30, 31, 33

Patton, George (General), 32, 95,
  98, 136, 137,

Pearl Harbor, 10-12, 14, 17,
  25-27, 47, 105

Peleliu Island, 75, 76, 82

Philadelphia, PA, 163, 166

Philco radio, 17

Philippines, 17-19, 22, 23, 46, 56,
  57, 165, 167, 170-172

Piute Indian, 27

Plymouth, England, 67

Poland, 87

Posey, Larry, 27, 31, 32

Posey, Rose, 32

Q

Quincy, IL, 47

Military Units

1st Armored Division, 166

1st Cavalry Division, 22

1st Marine Division, 76

2nd Infantry Regiment, 126

4th Constabulary Regiment, 177, 195

5th Infantry Division, 126

5th Infantry Regiment, 177

7th Cavalry Division, 52

11th Armored Division, 137

12th SS Panzer Division, 111

13th Airborne Division, 31

13th Armored Division, 145

XIXth Corps, 155

25th Panzer Grenadiers, 111

26th Infantry Division, 89, 95

29th Infantry Division, 69

30th Infantry Division, 72

32nd Infantry Division, 43,45,52,56,57,191

35th Cavalry Recon Sqdn, 164

39th Infantry Division, 82

45th Infantry Division, 115

65th Infantry Division, 135, 137

75th Infantry Division, 105

81st Infantry Division, 75,82

91st Bomb Group, 35

96th Bomb Group, 83

98th AAA Gun Battalion, 29

100th Infantry Division, 118, 122

104th Infantry Division, 87, 125

128th Infantry Regiment, 52

133rd Battalion, 164

261st Infantry Regiment, 135, 136

263rd Field Artillery Battalion 89

289th Infantry Regiment, 105, 107

321st Infantry Regiment, 76

322nd Bomb Group, 97, 104

322nd Infantry Regiment, 75, 76

332nd Fighter Group, 165

338th Bomb Squadron, 83

342nd Fighter Squadron, 169

348th Fighter Group, 169

390th Bomb Group, 147, 150, 152

399th Infantry Regiment, 117, 123

401st Bomb Squadron, 35

415th Infantry Regiment, 125

442nd Infantry Regiment, 120

450th Bomb Squadron, 98

515th Regiment, 31

568th Bomb Squadron, 147

747th Tank Battalion, 67-71

750th Port Battalion, 80

793rd Field Artillery Battalion, 155-157

3821 Truck Company, 164

6483rd Car Company, 164

The Author

Jerry Whiting is a South Dakota native and a graduate of the University of California, Santa Barbara, with a Bachelor of Arts Degree. He later earned a Master's Degree at John F. Kennedy University.

Jerry worked in Law Enforcement for 28 years in the San Francisco Bay Area, holding a variety of positions. During his unique career he had an opportunity to work with police departments in several European countries, studying tactics and procedures and spent a brief period as an observer with the Cheyenne River Sioux Tribal Police in South Dakota.

He has written two other books about World War II. *Don't Let the Blue Star Turn Gold: Downed Airmen in Europe in WW II*, is a series of true stories of American bomber crews shot down over occupied Europe, focusing on their fates after they were shot down. Jerry's first book, *I'm Off to War, Mother, But I'll Be Back: Reflections of a WWII Tail Gunner*, is a biography of his father's combat experiences over Europe and the promise he kept to return safely. For both of these books he traveled to Europe to locate eyewitnesses.

The author regularly assists other researchers and authors here and abroad and recently provided research assistance for three books about World War II, written and published in Italy. He has consulted with and provided training for the Department of Defense on MIA issues. He is currently the Historian for the 485th Bomb Group Association and served as publisher for their group history, *Missions by the Numbers: Combat Missions Flown by the 485th Bomb Group (H)*. Jerry has written articles for periodicals and magazines and he is often called upon as a guest speaker, where he always emphasizes the importance of preserving our rich American history and the lessons to be learned from it. He teaches part-time and he and his wife life in Walnut Creek, California.

You may contact the author directly for signed copies of books or with any questions or comments, at EAJWWhiting@aol.com.